Management Theory and Practice

Related titles in the series

Accounting
Advertising
Auditing
Book-keeping
Business and Commercial
 Law
Business and Enterprise
 Studies
Business French
Business German
Business Italian
Commerce
Cost and Management
 Accounting
Economics

Elements of Banking
Financial Management
Information Technology
Law
Management Theory and
 Practice
Marketing
Office Practice
Personnel Management
Psychiatry
Social Services
Statistics for Business
Teeline Shorthand
Typing

Management Theory and Practice

Rob Dixon

MADE SIMPLE
B O O K S

To Ann for all her patience

Made Simple
An imprint of Butterworth–Heinemann Ltd
Linacre House, Jordan Hill, Oxford OX2 8DP

 PART OF REED INTERNATIONAL BOOKS

OXFORD   LONDON   BOSTON
MUNICH   NEW DELHI   SINGAPORE   SYDNEY
TOKYO   TORONTO   WELLINGTON

First published 1991
Reprinted 1992

British Library Cataloguing in Publication Data
Dixon, Rob
  Management theory and practice
  – (Made simple series)
  I. Title   II. Series
  658.001

ISBN 0 7506 0137 X

Printed in England by Clays Ltd, St Ives plc

Contents

Preface

This book considers both the nature of management and the environment in which management operates. The requirements for effective, successful management techniques are explored; covering many areas from the need for planning and forecasting, leadership, motivation and communication, to control, decision-making and personnel management. There is also a short study of the basics of management information systems, their use and their purpose.

I would like to extend my gratitude to all those who have helped in the production of this book, particularly to Charlotte Ridings for her background research.

Rob Dixon

1
Introduction to management

This chapter will look at what management comprises and what functions and roles managers have to fulfil. The major schools of management theory are discussed, together with their relevance for today's managers.

1.1 What is management?

There is no generally accepted definition of management. Henri Fayol defined it as 'to forecast and plan, to organize, to command, to co-ordinate and to control' (Fayol 1948).

Peter Drucker, in *The Practice of Management* (1968), regarded management as 'the systematic organization of economic resources'. Essentially, management is about organizing people and resources productively, to the mutual benefit both of the organization as a whole and of the individual employees. The manager should see him/herself as facilitating this process.

Other writers, instead of trying to define management, have tried to produce an analysis of what managers do in practice. Mintzberg is among these. He lists the roles which managers consistently have to adopt in their jobs. These are:

1 *Entrepreneur*: the manager as planner and risk-taker.
2 *Resource allocater*: the manager as organizer and co-ordinator.
3 *Figurehead/leader*: the manager as motivator and co-ordinator.
4 *Liaison/disseminator*: the manager as co-ordinator and communicator.
5 *Monitor*: the manager as controller.

6 *Spokesman/negotiator*: the manager as motivator and communicator.
7 *Disturbance-handler*: the manager as motivator and co-ordinator.

From these it can be seen that a manager has to plan, take decisions, motivate, lead, organize, communicate, co-ordinate and control, and each of these aspects of a manager's job will be examined in later chapters.

Why is management important?

Management is essential for the success of a business, or any other enterprise. Drucker (1968) sums this up well:

> The manager is the dynamic, life-giving element in every business. Without his leadership the resources of production remain resources and never become production. In a competitive economy, above all, the quality and performance of the managers determine the success of a business, indeed they determine its survival. For the quality and performance of its managers is the only effective advantage an enterprise in a competitive economy can have.

1.2 Theories of management

Since the turn of the century writers on management and business have been propounding different theories about how to manage workers more efficiently and effectively. There are three main schools of management thought: the classical school, the human relations school, and the approach of the systems school. Although each approach reflects the thinking and attitudes of its time, they still have a lot of influence on current business methods and thought.

The classical school

Theorists of the classical school of management (the earliest of the schools) tried to form general principles of management which could be applied to all businesses and situations. Mass-production techniques were beginning to be widely used, and classical theorists sought to find the most economical way of producing the greatest number of products, through dividing tasks up into their constituent parts. The main writers of the classical school were F. W. Taylor, Henri Fayol, Frank and Lilian Gilbreth, and Henry Gantt.

F. W. Taylor and scientific management

Taylor's (1856–1915) scientific approach to management was concerned with the formal structure and activities of the organization, i.e. the span of managerial control, the division of work, etc. His ideas were developed mainly when Taylor was a manager at a steel company in the United States.

Taylor was mostly concerned with increasing efficiency in production methods, not only to lower costs and raise profits, but also to make it possible for workers to earn higher wages through their higher productivity. Taylor decided that the problem of productivity was a matter of ignorance on the part of both managers and workers. Unrealistic piece-rates of pay and production targets were set because managers had not analysed the work properly, and workers did not know how to carry out their jobs to maximize their efficiency. Taylor saw productivity as the answer to both higher wages and higher profits, and he believed that the application of scientific methods of job analysis, (determining the best way of doing the job), and training the workers in these new production methods, could yield this greater productivity.

The principles behind scientific management

The fundamental principles that Taylor thought underlied scientific management were set out in his book *The Principles of Scientific Management* (1911), and can be summarized as follows:

1   Replacing rules of thumb with a true science of work. Thus all knowledge kept in the heads of the workmen needed to be gathered and recorded by management. As Taylor wrote, 'every single subject, large and small,

becomes the question for scientific investigation, for reduction to law'.

2   Achieving the co-operation of human beings, rather than chaotic individualism. This referred specifically to relations between management and workers. In his book *Shop Management* (1903), Taylor wrote 'the relations between employers and men form without question the most important part of this art'.

3   The scientific selection and progressive development of workmen, i.e. workmen should be carefully trained, and given jobs to which they were best suited. They should be developed to the fullest extent possible for their own and the company's highest prosperity.

4   Working for maximum output rather than restricted output.

Other classical theorists

The classical theory of scientific management did not begin and end with Taylor. Early supporters and proponents of scientific management include Frank and Lilian Gilbreth and Henry Gantt.

Frank and Lilian Gilbreth

The Gilbreths' contribution to scientific management was in the field of motion study. Frank Gilbreth (1917) defined motion study as 'dividing the work into the most fundamental elements possible; studying these elements separately and in relation to one another; and from these studied elements, when timed, building methods of least waste' (*Applied Motion Study*).

One of the ways that motion study was carried out was through the use of flow process charts, which were used to analyse complete operations. Five symbols were used to analyse processes:

Operation
Inspection
Storage
Transportation
Delay

The basic elements of on-the-job movements were also broken down and analysed, with the help of symbols (called 'therbligs' – 'Gilbreth' almost backwards) such as:

Search ⟨◐⟩ Select ⟨◑⟩

Grasp ∩ Hold ⌒

Motion study was carried out in order to improve productivity and to reduce fatigue among workers. To achieve this latter aim the Gilbreths also introduced a shorter working day and rest periods, and contributory factors such as poor heating, lighting, and ventilation were studied. The Gilbreths, unlike Taylor, recognized that workers' output depended upon needs, attitudes and physical environment, as well as upon pay as a motivator.

Henry Gantt

Gantt, a colleague of Taylor, also helped to humanize scientific management. He applied a less detailed analysis to tasks than Taylor did, and he replaced the old piece-rate system of pay with a day-rate, with bonuses for those workers who met and exceeded the targets set. Workers were given more responsibility, as were the foremen – they received a bonus for each man who achieved the targets, and so were encouraged to help and train workers.

Gantt is most remembered for developing a type of bar chart which shows the time relation between 'events' in a production process. It was originally designed to show how far a task had been achieved in comparison to the optimum target set. See Figure 1.1.

Henri Fayol (1841–1925)

Henri Fayol was a French industrialist. Unlike Taylor, whose work was concentrated upon the shop floor, Fayol took a more comprehensive view of management's role throughout the organization, and popularized the concept of the 'universality of management principles': the idea that management should apply the same broad principles, no matter what sort of business is being managed. He is known

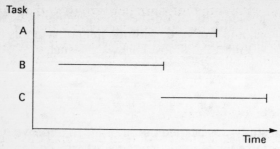

Figure 1.1 A Gantt chart

as the 'father of modern operational management theory', although his work was not published in the USA until 1949. His principles of management are still very much in use.

Fayol's functions of management

Fayol identified five elements or functions of management (see Figure 1.2):

1 Planning – selecting objectives and the strategies, policies, and procedures for achieving these objectives.
2 Organizing – the establishment of a structure of tasks which need to be performed to achieve the goals of an organization, grouping these tasks into jobs for an individual, delegating authority, providing for co-ordination and for systems of information and communication.
3 Commanding – giving instructions to subordinates.
4 Co-ordinating – this is usually known today more as motivating. Management harmonizes the activities of the

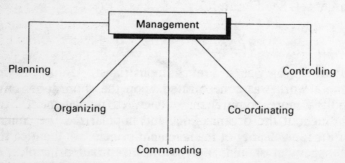

Figure 1.2 Fayol's elements of management

groups within the organization so that they are all working towards the goals of the organization.
5 Controlling – measuring and correcting the performance of workers to ensure it meets the requirements of the planned performance.

Fayol's principles of management

From these five elements Fayol then developed his fourteen management principles:

1 Division of work – specialization of tasks which, Fayol argued, was necessary for greater efficiency and productivity.
2 Authority and responsibility – authority is the right to issue commands; responsibility is related to this authority and, indeed, arises out of it.
3 Discipline – Fayol declared that discipline required good superiors at all levels.
4 Unity of command – this means that employees should receive orders from one superior only.
5 Unity of direction – according to this principle, each group of activities with the same objective must have one head and one plan.
6 Subordination – of the individual to the general interest.
7 Remuneration – remuneration and methods of payment should be fair and afford the maximum possible satisfaction to employees and employer alike.
8 Centralization – this refers to the extent to which authority is concentrated or dispersed.
9 Scalar chain – Fayol conceived this as a 'chain of superiors' from the highest to the lowest ranks, which, while not to be departed from needlessly, should be short-circuited if it would be detrimental to follow it scrupulously.
10 Order – this is essentially a principle of organization in the arrangement of things and people.
11 Equity – this principle held that management should judge things and people with fairness.
12 Stability of tenure – by this Fayol meant that no manager can function effectively if he is dependent

upon short-term reviews of salary or contract to continue his career progress or to keep his job. Rather,
there ought to be a proper period of training and
settling down, and at all times the promise of freedom
from interference.

13   Initiative – Fayol suggested that this be encouraged to
the full.

14   *Esprit de corps* – this principle suggests that a good
team spirit and morale be built up by management
among the workers.

The achievements of the classical school

Classical theories of scientific management brought a far
more formal and rational approach to management than
there had been before, and there is no doubt that the
improvements made in working practices and methods due
to the introduction of quantitative work study did achieve
the vast increases in productivity (and therefore workers'
pay) which they were meant to.

However, this approach to management does have serious
drawbacks. It led to tasks being reduced to their simplest,
smallest elements, which meant that work became increasingly boring, repetitive, and de-skilled. It also assumed that
workers were only motivated by money, by tying pay to
output so closely.

Classical management theories still have a great deal of
influence, with their emphasis on work and time and motion
studies, and the continued use of fragmented, minimalist
work, especially in mass-production factories such as car-
manufacturing plants, although the dehumanizing effect of
this is now being recognized and some companies are trying
to do something to reduce it.

The human relations school

The classical approach to management focuses upon the
structure of the organization, rather than the workers in it.
The human relations or behavioural school, in contrast,
considers the people within the organization – their social
needs, motivation and behaviour. This new approach really
began in earnest during the 1920s and 1930s, when the

classical theories which were prevalent were failing to halt falling production levels and standards.

Elton Mayo (1880–1949), and his studies into the working conditions and levels of productivity at the Hawthorne plant of the Western Electric Company in Chicago, between 1927 and 1932, was the first real advocate of the behavioural approach to management. However, there were one or two earlier writers who had begun to pave the way for such thinking. For example, French sociologist Emile Durkheim (1825–1917) recognized that groups of people tended to form their own values, rules and norms of behaviour, and were able to subordinate the behaviour of individual members of the group to these group values and norms.

Mary Parker Follett (1868–1933), expanded on Durkheim's work. She pointed out the importance for managers to understand how and why social groups formed and to reconcile the needs of individual workers with those of these groups.

Elton Mayo and the Hawthorne studies

The Hawthorne studies established once and for all that workers could become highly motivated by being part of a social/work group, and through being consulted by management as to changes in work practices, and so forth. These social groups were also seen to have a great influence on workers' behaviour, and were capable of working against the organization's goals and production targets, as well as helping motivate their members to work harder and produce more.

Other proponents of the human relations approach to management include Abraham Maslow, McGregor, Herzberg. and Rensis Likert. Their theories focus upon the motivation of the individual, and are discussed later on.

The systems school

The systems theory of management developed in the 1950s and 1960s. The approach attempts to explain and predict the behaviour of the organization by the study of the complete organization – its people, structure, environment and technology – not just by a single aspect of it, as both the human relations and classical schools do. The organization is seen as a collection of interacting parts, which have to be viewed as a whole.

Systems can be either open or closed. A closed system is one that is self-supporting, and which does not interact with the environment that it exists in. In contrast, open systems, such as business organizations, do interact with their environment. A business receives inputs from its environment (e.g. people, finance, raw materials), which it uses to produce products, which are then sold back into the environment. See Figure 1.3

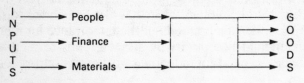

Figure 1.3   Open systems

The contribution of systems theory

The systems approach has contributed to the development of management thinking in three major ways:

1   It has shown that management has to consider all the variables in the organization – people, structure, technology, environment – as a cohesive whole, and not as separate items.
2   It has drawn attention to the importance of planning, as it has shown that formal organizations need a purpose and therefore it is vital for managers to plan.
3   The achievement of the plan depends on monitoring actual results against planned results, and correcting any deviations, i.e. control.

The contingency approach to management

The contingency approach to management developed out of the systems approach. Systems theory emphasizes the complex nature of the organization, with its different contributory variables. Contingency theory develops this view of the complex organization. Using this approach, management style and organizational structure should reflect and change with the changing environment the company finds itself in.

Unlike the other management schools, the contingency approach does not believe that there is one best way of management, and that the principles of this can be applied under all circumstances. Instead the contingency theorists take perhaps a more realistic approach – that the most appropriate method of management will change over time as the circumstances of the organization change. Managers should use whatever method is best for the company at that particular time.

The work of contingency theorists (such as Woodward, and Burns and Stalker) will be looked at in more detail when the effects of factors like size and technology on organizational structure are discussed.

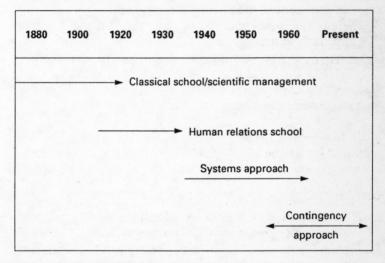

Figure 1.4. Development of management theory

1.3 Summary

1 Management can be defined as deciding what has to be done and organizing others to do it.
2 Theories about management have developed from the

one dimensional classical (scientific) and human relations approaches, through to the multi-dimensional approach of the systems school, and finally to contingency theory of flexible management, responding to changes in the environment by changing the management approach used. See Figure 1.4.

1.4 Quick questions

1 According to Mintzberg, what are the roles that managers have to adopt in their jobs?
2 List the principles behind Taylor's 'scientific management'.
3 List Fayol's fourteen universal principles of management.
4 How important were the Hawthorne studies to the development of management thought?
5 What do you understand by the phrase 'systems approach to management'?
6 How does the contingency approach to management develop and build upon the systems approach?

2
The managerial environment

This chapter looks at the internal and external business environment, and how it affects both the organization itself and managers in their work.

2.1 The external business environment

The environment in which a company operates constantly influences its management. The different elements of this environment will both act as constraints on the business' operations and will present the company with new markets and opportunities to exploit.

However, it is not always clear where the organization ends and its external environment begins. This is because the organization imports resources from the environment, such as raw materials, finance, employees, etc., and because the activities of the organization may be subject to 'rights' or claims of interest groups in the environment.

Therefore the boundaries between the two are blurred: employees simultaneously interact with, and are a part of, the environment outside the company. Nor are the boundaries between the organization and the environment static, for they are based on relationships rather than things. Thus while certain fixed elements, such as physical location, do have some impact on an organization's limits, it is management decisions that really determine where the organization ends and the environment begins. It can be said that different workers and their tasks are at the company's boundaries, depending on the activity at the time; sometimes it is the switchboard operator, while at other times it is the managing director.

2.2 Elements of the external environment

The external environment is made up of a number of different elements. There is the economic environment, the technological environment, the political and legal environment, and the social/cultural environment.

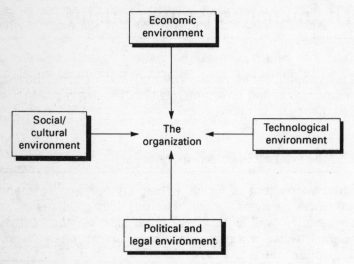

Figure 2.1   The organization and the environment

The economic environment

The economic environment has an effect on the organization for two reasons:

1 It relates to the effect of price level changes on the company.
2 The level of economic activity indicates the general likelihood of consumer incomes either rising or falling. This will affect both company sales, wage rates and costs.

The economic environment comprises several elements, which all have either a greater or lesser effect on business and organizations:

(a) *The supplier*, who provides the organization with raw materials and components for its needs. The organization has to purchase these at a price (and quality) which it can afford and still make a profit from selling the finished goods.

(b) *Customers* form another part of the economic environment, and can influence the organization in that their demands determine what an organization produces in the way of goods and services, and the price at which they can be sold.

(c) *The government* is a particularly important element in the economic environment. Government fiscal and monetary policies influence the organization in relation to the cost and availability of credit, the level of taxation, interest rates, and exchange rates (if the company exports its goods).

(d) *The investor*. Business confidence and the willingness of investors to lend are closely linked to expectations on the future level of economic activity. Thus the state of the general economic environment determines the ability of businesses to borrow money for investment purposes.

(e) *Competitors*, who are simply a 'threat' in the economic environment.

The technological environment

The technological environment and developments in technology have a great influence on the ways in which a company operates. Computers have revolutionized product design and manufacture, for example, the introduction of sophisticated automated or robotic machinery in the car manufacturing industry can now equip a group of people to do what required a mini-organization to do even just a few years ago. It has also changed work patterns away from the assembly line and back to the 'gang' or 'work group'.

Advances in technology have also made possible the opening up of new markets which were previously unexploited, either because the technical 'know-how' was lacking, or because the costs were prohibitive. Oil and gas exploration offshore is just one example of this.

Although technical developments and innovations can

present enormous opportunities for companies, the rapid pace of change in this field does also mean that, unless businesses are careful, they can find their products and manufacturing processes becoming obsolete very quickly. It is vital therefore for companies to pay a lot of attention to monitoring the technological environment and to forecasting possible medium- to long-term changes in it.

The legal environment

The legal environment is a very important external constraint on organizations. The law sets out the operating conditions of most businesses, ranging from specific bans on certain kinds of behaviour, to regulations requiring the reporting of income and staffing at various times of the year. Companies have to comply with laws setting minimum health and safety standards; laws on employment practices; laws banning discrimination on grounds of race, religion, sex, and marital status; trade union laws, and so on.

The legal environment, however, cannot be considered in isolation from the political environment, which brings about the enactment of new laws.

The political environment

The political environment, consisting of the government and parliament in the UK, as well as the European Commission, Council and European Parliament, pass the many, many laws and regulations which affect the way organizations function. This network of laws, regulations, directives and court decisions presents a complex environment for all companies to operate in. The way in which an organization responds to this environment may well determine its success or failure.

The organization can respond to these constraints by studying the prospective legislation, in order to develop a business strategy which will deal with the new legal framework within the necessary time span. For example, car manufacturers who developed engines with the capacity to run on both leaded and lead-free petrol, before leaded petrol has been either totally banned or priced out of the market in favour of unleaded fuel, have neutralized this potential threat to their business.

Political pressure

It must be noted, however, that there is a political influence upon the organization and its management regardless of any legal obligations. For example, strong political pressures brought by conservation groups concerned about potential pollution has affected industrial companies, e.g. chemical manufacturers, independently of any legal ramifications.

The political environment is very closely linked with the social environment. Often laws are passed as the result of social pressure on the government. In addition, the ability of political parties to make laws depends upon popular acceptance of their social and economic doctrines at the polls.

The social/cultural environment

The social or cultural environment is the final major element making up the external business environment. It consists of the attitudes, customs, beliefs, education, etc., of people and society at large. The most important determining factors of this social environment are the class, culture, age, sex and political beliefs of the people in it. This environment has a significant influence upon the organization and the way it is managed, as the organization is made up of people who are part of this external environment, as well as part of the organization.

Closely linked with the social environment is what may be termed the 'ethical environment', which consists of a set of well-established rules of personal and organizational behaviour and values. The ethical environment of organizations refers to justice, respect for the law and a moral code. The conduct of any company will be measured against ethical standards by the customers, suppliers and the general public with whom the company deals. The problem with 'moral ethics', however, is that the organization's view of the world may not always be in accordance with society's normal codes of morality.

2.3 Types of environment

The different elements which make up the business environment tend to relate to each other in different ways, bringing about a particular set of circumstances in the environment which the organization has to react to. Emery and Trist (1965) referred to this as the 'casual texture' of the environment.

Environments are considered to be made up of various 'good' and 'bad' elements, which act upon the organization. Emery and Trist identified four types of environment, each of which affect the business and its management in very different ways:

1   *The placid randomized environment* – an environment in which the good and bad elements are relatively unchanging in themselves and randomly distributed. In such an environment the organization need hardly plan a strategy as such, and is able to act purely on a tactical basis.

2   *The placid clustered environment* – an environment in which the good and bad elements are not randomly distributed, but relate to each other and hang together in certain ways. An organization must respond to this kind of environment with strategic, long-term planning rather than merely short-term tactics.

3   *Disturbed–reactive environment* – in this type of environment there is more than one organization of the same kind; indeed, the dominant characteristic of this type of environment is the existence of a number of similar organizations. In this type of environment each organization does not simply have to take account of the others when they meet at random, but also has to consider that what it knows may also be known by its competitors.

4   *Turbulent environment* – in this environment, dynamic processes, which create significant variances for the component organizations, arise from the field itself. The organization operating in this environment thus faces great uncertainty, with the consequences of any actions becoming increasingly unpredictable.

2.4 The internal environment/culture of the organization

The culture of the organization is the unique configuration of values, beliefs, behavioural patterns, and so on which characterize the manner in which groups and individual employees work together in order to achieve their objectives. The individuality of businesses is therefore expressed in terms of their differing cultures.

The major four types of organizational culture have been identified by Charles Handy (1984) as the power culture, the role culture, the task culture, and the person culture.

The power culture

In this culture power rests with a central figure who exercises control through the selection of key individuals. An organization with this kind of culture operates with few rules, and decisions are often taken on the outcome of a balance of influence rather than in accordance with logic or procedure.

A strength of the power culture, and the organization based upon it, is that it has the ability to move quickly and react well to any threat. However, whether the company does move quickly – or in the right direction – depends upon the person or persons in control. Therefore the success of companies with a power culture depends largely upon the quality of the individuals in control. Thus the power culture puts a tremendous amount of faith in the individual, and is often found in new companies controlled by their entrepreneurial founders.

Size and growth do pose problems for power cultures. Often successful business with power cultures and dynamic founders grow comparatively quickly, and become too big to be manageable by one person. If such a company is to remain a cohesive, controllable entity, it should really create other, subordinate, organizations, or risk becoming a victim of its own success.

The role culture

The organization based upon the role culture is structured according to functions or expertise, e.g. the finance department, the personnel department. Each of these functions is strong in its own right, but they are co-ordinated by a small group of senior management by means of a set of rules and procedures, such as:

1   Procedures for tasks/roles, e.g. job descriptions.
2   Procedures for communications.
3   Rules for settling disputes.

Rules and procedures are therefore the major source of influence in the role culture, which is better known perhaps as bureaucracy.

Job v individual

In the role culture the role or job is all important, the individual being of a secondary consideration. People are selected in order to perform a role, and that role is usually described in such a way that a range of individuals could fill it. Whether the organization is efficient therefore depends not so much on an individual's qualities – as in the power culture – but on the rationality of the allocation of work and responsibility.

Role culture and environment

The success of a role culture organization depends upon a stable environment. It will then provide security and predictability in terms of the acquisition and promotion of specialist expertise without risks. This of course will not be attractive to the eager, ambitious individual, or the person who is seeking personal power, or who is interested in results rather than methods.

Role cultures are slow to see any need for change and are slow to change even if that need is perceived. Therefore the organization based upon the role culture will be found where economies of scale are more important than flexibility, or where technical expertise and depth of specialization are more important than product innovation or product cost.

The task culture

The task culture places emphasis on accomplishing the task or the project. To do this it seeks to bring together the appropriately qualified personnel in a team, and supply them with the resources they need to accomplish their given job. The task culture provides the team members with a substantial amount of control over their work, and they also enjoy mutual respect within the group, a respect based upon capability rather than age or rank. The task culture harnesses the unity of this team, with its aim of completing a particular project, in order to improve efficiency and to identify the individual with the objectives of the organization.

Top management maintains control in the task culture, because it has the power to allocate projects, people and resources. But this is not control on a day-to-day basis; team members keep substantial control over their work, and indeed any attempt by senior management to exercise closer everyday control would not be acceptable in this culture.

When resources are not available, however, management often feels a need to interfere in the control of the project teams' work. Team leaders also start to vie for the scarce resources, and consequently the task culture begins to change to a power culture.

Flexibility of the task culture

The task culture is very adaptable and is therefore appropriate where flexibility and sensitivity to the market or to the environment are important, i.e. where the market is competitive and the product life is short. Conversely, it is not suitable in situations which require economies of scale or great depths of expertise.

The task culture is popular with managers. According to Handy it is 'the culture most in tune with current ideologies of change and adaptation, individual freedom and low status differentials'. Even so, the task culture is not always the most appropriate culture for the prevailing climate and the technology.

The person culture

In the person culture the purpose of the organization's existence is to serve the individual. The individual is therefore the central point in the person culture. Organizations based upon the person culture are rare – usually they are family firms. Instead one tends to find within another culture a person whose behaviour and attitudes reveal a preference for the person culture. A much used example of this is the person- culture-oriented professor working within a role culture. The professor does what he/she must, teaching when required, in order to retain his/her position in the organization. Essentially, however, he/she regards the organization as a base on which to build his/her own career and interests. These may indirectly add interest and value to the organization, though that would not be the professor's primary motive.

Factors influencing culture

The culture of an organization is a matter of choice. There are a number of factors which determine an organization's choice of culture:

1 *Size* is a very important variable influencing an organization's choice of culture. The larger an organization, the greater the tendency towards formalization and the development of specialized groups requiring systematic co-ordination. Therefore size generally inclines an organization towards a role culture.
2 *History and ownership*. Where there is centralized ownership, e.g. in family firms, there is a tendency towards a power culture. Diffused ownership allows diffused influence, based on alternative sources of power.
3 *Technology*. In general, routine programmable operations are more suitable to a role culture than to any of the other cultures, as are high cost technologies which require close monitoring and supervision and depth of expertise, and technologies where there are economies of scale available. However, where organizations are engaged in unit production and non-continuous oper-

ations, power or task cultures are more suitable, as they are when technology is changing rapidly.

4 *Goals and objectives*. Quality objectives can generally be more easily monitored in role cultures, while growth objectives are usually more appropriate in power or task cultures.

5 *The environment* is another important factor influencing the choice of culture. An unstable, changing environment requires an adaptable, responsive culture, i.e. a task culture, whereas a more stable environment may incline an organization towards a role culture.

6 *The people*. The availability of suitably qualified people is a significant factor in any choice of culture. The individual preferences of key people in the organization will also have a large say in determining the dominant culture, irrespective of what it actually should be for the good of the company.

Differentiation

An organization might have a structure which reflects a single culture; on the other hand, different structures reflecting different cultures might exist side by side in separate departments of the same organization. This is known as 'differentiation', and should help the organization to adapt to changes in its external environment better and more quickly than it perhaps would if it had just one organizational culture. However, to be successful, differentiation has to be both co-ordinated and integrated, or else there is a danger that the company's employees will not work together towards any common aim or goal.

2.5 Summary

1 The organization is affected by its external environment because, as an open system, it interacts with it, taking inputs from the environment and returning goods and people out into it again.

2 The external environment consists of economic, technological, legal, political, and social/ethical elements.

3 These elements present both business opportunities and

threats, and combine to form different environment types: placid randomized, placid clustered, disturbed–reactive, and turbulent.
4   There are four types of internal organizational culture: the power culture, the role culture, the task culture, and the person culture.
5   Organizational culture choice is influenced by a company's size, previous ownership, the technology it uses, its objectives, the type of environment it operates in, and by the people in it.
6   An organization may have more than one culture structure at the same time – this is called differentiation.

2.6 Quick questions

1   Outline the various elements which make up an organization's external environment.
2   How does the external business environment affect the organization?
3   What are the four types of environment identified by Emery and Trist?
4   Explain what is meant by the 'culture' of an organization.
5   What factors influence this organizational culture?

2.7 Exercise

Organizations may have either power, task, role or person cultures, or they may be differentiated. Take a company or organization with which you are familiar and consider:

(i)   what culture predominates in this organization?
(ii) what degree of differentiation (if any) exists between different parts of the organization?
(iii) what possible improvements in the culture or structure of the company can you suggest?

3
Planning and forecasting

In this chapter the different types and levels of planning a company can undertake, and their integration, are looked at. In addition, we consider the parts of the planning process, and the role that forecasting plays in reducing uncertainty about future changes in the business' external environment.

3.1 Introduction

Planning is a fundamental function of management. It consists of selecting strategies from among alternative possible courses of action, both for the enterprise as a whole and for every department or section within it. This requires the company's objectives to be defined and departmental goals to be set in order to meet those objectives, and finding ways to achieve them.

Planning is, in effect, deciding in advance what do do, how to do it, when to do it, and who is to do it. Without planning, an organization would not really know if it was accomplishing its purpose. How can someone tell if they have reached their destination, if they don't know where they are heading for when they set out?

Forecasting is a vital part of planning, as any longer range plans need to take possible developments in technology, markets, products and manufacturing processes, etc., into account.

Management uses planning for four important reasons:

1 To offset uncertainty and change.
2 To focus attention on objectives.

3   To gain economical operation.
4   To facilitate control.

3.2 Types of planning

There are several different types or levels of planning. These vary from each other in both their time-scale and the amount of detail that they go into. Basically, the longer the period of time covered, the less detailed the plans, and the greater the degree of uncertainty and risk attached to them. It also follows that the longer the period covered by the plans, the more senior the managers who make them are. See Table 3.1.

Table 3.1

Plans	Time-scale	Degree of detail	Seniority of managers
Strategic	5–10 yrs	vague	Board level
Management	12 mths	high	Dept heads
Operational	up to 1 week	very	Supervisors

The co-ordination and implementation of these plans are usually referred to as corporate planning – planning for the company as a whole to ensure that all departmental long-term objectives are compatible and do not conflict with each other. The relations between these different planning levels are shown in Figure 3.1.

Figure 3.1   Planning levels

Corporate planning

Drucker defined corporate planning as:

> The continuous process of making present risk-taking decisions systematically and with the greatest knowledge of their futurity; organizing systematically the efforts needed to carry out these decisions, and measuring the results of these decisions against the expectations through organized, systematic feedback.

The aim of corporate planning is to define and clarify the objectives of the organization as a whole. It calls for an appraisal of the major strengths and weaknesses within the company, and an appraisal of the opportunities and threats posed by the external environment, both of which will have an effect on the company's achievement of its objectives. Corporate planning also needs sufficiently detailed operational plans, which can be amended if necessary, to help ensure that the company's objectives are achieved. The success of corporate planning requires accurate, concise, relevant and up-to-date information.

Why corporate planning is needed

A corporate planning system, co-ordinating the plans for the entire business over several years, may be introduced for the following reasons:

1 It is important that an organization identifies its objectives and also any gaps that exist between its current supply of goods and services and the demands of the market.
2 Competition for scarce resources within an organization increases with the size of the organization, and this creates a need for central planning and control, as opposed to planning by individual departments or managers.
3 The ever-quickening pace of change requires that organizations adapt and react to change *corporately* rather than on an individual departmental basis.

Strategic planning

Strategic planning is the long-range planning part of corporate planning. It comprises establishing where the company is liable to be in 5–10 years' time, in view of any possible forecasted changes in its business environment, and, with this in mind, developing long-term plans which will allow the company to achieve its objectives. Examples of long-term strategies are the development of new products, the opening up of new markets, and the expansion into different areas of business.

Management planning

This is a lower level of planning, and might be termed intermediate planning. Management planning is concerned with the following:

1 Determining the structure of the organization.
2 Establishing functional and departmental objectives in line with corporate policies.
3 Deciding upon product sale mixes.
4 Formulating financial budgets and planning staff requirements.

Operational planning

This is the lowest level of planning, in which the line manager and management at supervisory and foreman levels set specific tasks to achieve key targets. Some targets are expressed in financial terms. Others are expressed in measures such as output per employee, percentage utilization of machines, cost level etc. Once these targets have been set, they are monitored and revised as necessary. If revisions are made, then the whole plan is altered accordingly, so that the long-term perspective is maintained but the entire plan is kept up-to-date.

3.3 The planning process

The operation of most organizations is based on plans and planning. This does not just happen, however. It is the result of a planning process, which is quite often lengthy and needs considerable thought. The process in corporate planning is designed so that the organization knows the following:

1 Its main objectives and why it exists.
2 What opportunities and threats are presented to it by the external environment.
3 Its own internal strengths and weaknesses.
4 How to establish a base for its strategic and operational planning.
5 How to establish policies which will allow employees to pursue the organization's objectives.

The planning process can be divided into several stages.

Setting objectives

The first stage in planning is the identification and description of the company's objectives. Objectives are the ends towards which the activities and operations of an organization are directed; they give purpose and meaning to the organization's existence. For example, for a public service, such as British Rail, this could be 'To provide a service for the community'.

There are two types of objective: those that lay down the objective and purpose of the company (as above); and those that set out the company's long-term aims, which define what sort of organization the company means to be in the future, and what kind of business it expects to be conducting.

The traditional objective for companies is to maximize profits. However, this is fairly unrealistic, not least because it is very difficult to judge whether or not profits have been maximized – a project which was not undertaken may have yielded greater returns than one which was chosen in its place. Maximizing profits in the short term may also reduce shareholders' returns in the long term. The traditional profit objective is thus usually amended to the achievement of sufficient profits to ensure the company's survival and growth, and to give shareholders an acceptable return on their investment.

According to what has been called the behavioural theory of the firm (put forward by Cyert and March), the organization is made up of a coalition of different interest groups, or stakeholders, such as the managers, employees, shareholders, customers, and so on. The company's long-term aims are therefore established over a variety of areas, such as market share, sales growth, public responsibility, to satisfy the interests of these different groups. The different objectives occur because the owners of companies often are not the same people who control businesses in practice, owing to the emergence of multiple shareholders and professional managers. However, these different objectives must still be compatible, because an organization cannot operate in several directions at the same time.

Frequently set objectives

According to Drucker in *The Practice of Management*, most organizations set objectives in the following areas, which seek to meet the needs of all the different stakeholders:

1 *Profitability*. The primary objective of a profit-earning business is growth in earnings per share. In working out the long-term objectives for growth of earnings, consideration has to be given to such aspects as net dividends, taxation, inflation and profit, etc.
2 *Innovation*. The board of directors must determine whether the organization intends to be an innovator in technology and products, or whether it will follow the lead of other companies. Its ability to innovate depends upon the technical and creative resources at its disposal. A technical policy must be devised and objectives defined for research and development, in conjunction with marketing and manufacturing objectives.
3 *Market standing and position*. Marketing objectives include such matters as what products are to be sold in various markets, whether the organization is to be a market leader in innovation and pricing, the degree of market penetration it seeks, and the standards of service required.
4 *Productivity*. Objectives are expressed in terms of output

per employee, and output in relation to plant, material yields, and costs.

5 *Resources*. Most organizations have objectives relating to both financial and physical resources.

6 *Management performance and development*. Objectives are also set with regard to organization and development quality, availability of management, measures of performance, etc.

7 *Employee performance*. Here objectives cover the development of management/worker relations.

8 *Public and social responsibility*. Objectives here include the preservation and improvement of the environment, consumer protection, improvements in conditions of work, sponsorship and participation in local activities, etc.

The objectives set must be definite and specific enough for management to be able to translate them into policies and plans for action.

Internal and external appraisal

Thorough appraisal of the company's internal and external environment is vital for the formulation of strategic plans. The appraisals should be concerned with identifying the few areas considered to be crucial for the company's success or failure over the coming 5–10 years. They should identify the business's strengths and weaknesses, and the opportunities and threats posed by its environment: the process is sometimes referred to as SWOT analysis.

Internal appraisal

The purpose of an internal appraisal is to identify what functions the organization is good or bad at undertaking, and to forecast what the results might be if the company continues as it is, without exploiting its strengths and reducing its weaknesses. The areas which should be examined objectively include:

1 *Finance* – present and projected performance, compared with past performance trends, and inter-firm or industrial

averages, to show relative strength of company; the effectiveness of routine financial reporting and budgeting.

2 *Products* – scope, range, prices, age, quality, durability and appeal of the company's products; plus the company's record of introducing successful new goods.

3 *Markets* – the range of markets the company sells in; each market share and rate of growth; market composition by customer type, geographical area, etc.

4 *Research and development* – comparison with competitors; success rate of developing new ideas, etc.

5 *Production and supply* – trends in output compared to capacity; productivity; quality of goods, plant and equipment; whether the sources of raw materials are good in terms of delivery times, etc; the efficiency of stock control.

6 *Personnel* – age, ability and skills of the workforce; the adequacy of staff training; the state of industrial relations.

7 *Management* – age, ability and skills of the managers; plus promotion policies, and provisions for management succession, especially to senior management posts.

8 *Organizational structure* – the suitability of the organization's structure for the company's business, in terms of channels of communication, lines of authority, etc.

It is important that the internal appraisal concentrates upon the future and the potential of the organization rather than upon past mistakes and problems. The review should also be objective, with plans for improving problem areas being put forward.

External appraisal

An external appraisal considers the outside environment in which the company operates, and tries to forecast possible changes in it which could either be a serious threat to the organization (in which case the organization can take action to lessen their impact), or developments which can be exploited for the good of the business. See Figure 3.2.

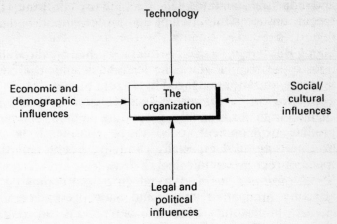

Figure 3.2 Environmental influences on the organization

The organization should assess a number of areas within the environment during an external appraisal:

1 *Economic environment.* A multi-national company will need to assess the international economic situation, while a company trading exclusively in one country will need to focus its appraisal on the domestic economic situation. Both will need to collect and assess information which is relevant to their marketing plans, e.g. changes in the gross domestic product, changes in fixed capital information, changes in consumer income and expenditure, and population growth.

2 *Political environment.* An external appraisal will need to assess the political environment within which the organization operates. For example, a company operating in Hong Kong will need to assess and take into consideration the uncertain political future of that place when formulating its plans. On a more mundane level, assessment of the political environment will include areas such as government action in terms of taxation and subsidies, spending, and import duties.

3 *Legal environment.* Consideration must be given to the legal environment in making an external appraisal. For example, legal changes resulting from the establishment of the single European market relating to competition, patents, sale of goods, pollution, working regulations

and industrial standards will affect the organization. The recent unsuccessful attempt to change the law with regard to Sunday trading, by the introduction of the Shops Bill in the House of Commons, has drawn attention to the way in which the legal environment affects those organizations engaged in the retail trade.

4   *Technological environment*. Technological factors, e.g. changes in material supply, processing methods and new product development, need to be considered in an external appraisal especially carefully, because of the speed of recent technological change.

5   *Social environment*. The social environment has been affecting companies more and more recently, and changes in customer tastes and perceptions can have a major impact on a business. For example, the growing awareness of environmental matters has led to many companies having to alter their production processes and image. Future changes in the physical make-up of society e.g. demographic trends, will also affect companies.

Forecasting changes

An external appraisal must not only assess the present situation within the environment and the ongoing changes, but also seek to ascertain any likely future changes. This forecasting of environmental change is fraught with difficulties because of unknown factors, including the behaviour of variables and totally unpredictable events.

Technological forecasting is a relatively new technique which attempts to estimate the future level of technology that will have an impact on the corporate plan. The actual methods used in environmental forecasting range from fairly simple correlation methods to the building up of an econometric matrix. In between, there are mathematical models of possible business scenarios to try to predict the probability of certain events occurring, plus corporate models and game plans. All forecasting has been revolutionized in recent years by the widespread use of computer technology. Computers have made it a lot easier to manipulate large sets of figures than before, and of course have generally made it easier for companies to generate acccurate data and reasonable predictions.

All long-term planning has to be based on supposition and predictions of possible events. Forecasting will help a little to reduce the uncertainty surrounding the future, but it has to be remembered that strategic plans are based on the 'most likely' outcome of events. Risk is reduced, but is certainly always present.

Evaluation of alternatives

The third stage in the planning process is choosing and evaluating alternative ways of achieving the company's aims and of taking advantage of strengths and opportunities revealed in the SWOT analysis, while minimizing the effect of weaknesses and threats. For example, a company may aim to fill its senior management positions through internal appointments, but may presently find that, although it has very adequate middle and junior managers, there are not many outstanding candidates for the higher positions. It could seek to remedy this by either improving its management development programme, by improving its junior and middle management recruitment and selection procedures, or both. The problem rarely lies in finding alternatives but in reducing the number of alternatives to those promising the most fruitful possibilities, and then analysing those alternatives.

The alternative strategies have to be investigated to see how they will affect the company. They should be analysed in terms of whether or not the company will be better off after the change than it was before, the affect of the change on the company's profits year by year, and whether the company will be able to raise sufficient capital to meet all the anticipated expenditure required under the proposal. The alternatives of course must also be evaluated in the light of all the organization's objectives, remembering in doing so that one objective may create a constraint on other objectives. This may mean that the objectives might have to be put into some sort of order of importance, and the strategy which helps fulfil an important objective should be chosen in preference to another plan which fulfils a lesser objective if there is a clash of interests.

There are three reasons why alternative strategies are often not evaluated in sufficient depth by companies:

1 The uncertainty inherent in forecasting is assumed to make any detailed evaluation invalid.
2 The large numbers of available alternatives make the task very daunting.
3 The amount of time needed for detailed evaluation is regarded as excessive.

However, if alternatives are not evaluated properly, it negates the whole planning process.

The need to evaluate regularly alternative ways of achieving given objectives is generally most keenly felt by private sector organizations whose market is under constant threat from competitors. The need also exists, however, in the public sector, especially now budget cutbacks require all managers to make the most efficient use of the resources under their control.

A strategic planning flow chart is shown in Figure 3.3.

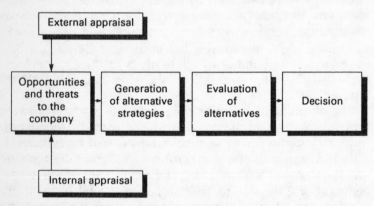

Figure 3.3 Strategic planning flow chart

Formulating plans

After the alternative strategies have been evaluated and a choice made, a point is reached at which the strategy is translated into detailed plans. At this stage the broad implications for the various parts of the organization are made clear; specific year-by-year targets for each manager are laid down, perhaps with an indication of the reasons for any changes from the current targets, and the available resources are specified.

Ranges of plans

The degree of detail contained in these plans varies considerably from one organization to another. At one extreme some private sector groups, such as GEC, lay down financial targets for each company within the group and then give the companies considerable freedom as to the policies that they adopt to reach those targets. At the other extreme, public sector organizations tend to be much more specific about the policies to be adopted and the resources available, with detailed budgets being established for equipment, materials and staff of various kinds.

The components of the plans will be in terms of particular products for various markets and will lay down resource requirements in order to achieve their implementation. The plans may include areas such as image as well as products and markets, although these latter factors usually dominate.

The co-ordination of short- and long-range plans

As we have seen, the strategic part of an organization's corporate plan will outline broadly the means by which objectives are to be achieved. This is then broken down into management and operational plans with key targets. Often a serious error is made in that these shorter-range plans are made without reference to the long-range plans. The integration of the two types is very important; no short-range target should be set unless it contributes to the achievement of the relevant long-range plan and objectives. Sometimes short-range decisions not only fail to contribute to the long-range plans but actually impede, or cause changes in, the strategic plans. Responsible managers should continually scrutinize immediate decisions to ascertain whether they contribute to the organization's long-range plans, and subordinate managers should be briefed regularly on the long-term objectives and plans of the company, so that they will make consistent short-term decisions.

3.4 The role of budgets in the planning process

Budgets are an important feature of planning because, in effect, they force managers to plan. A budget sets out expected results in numerical terms and provides an indication of how resources need to be allocated to certain activities over a specified period of time, in order to achieve set targets. The process of setting a budget, at least annually, forces managers to consider and plan their goals and objectives.

How budgets help planning

1 Budgets have to be prepared throughout the organization and all managers are concerned in this process. This means that every manager participates in, and, it is hoped, becomes committed to, planning.
2 They facilitate the co-ordination of activities on an organization-wide basis.
3 They quantify targets and communicate those targets to the individuals expected to fulfil them.
4 They provide for a comparison or monitoring of actual results with budgeted results, and therefore facilitate control. Any significant variance between planned results and actual results is investigated, and either the plan or variation is corrected.

Budgets and control

If budgets are to be effective, then the managers responsible for their implementation need to take part in their preparation. Just as planning is a prerequisite for control, so budgets are an essential tool for management control. The control function of budgets, and the whole area of control (together with budgetary methods), are discussed in Chapter 8, but we can briefly outline here the part control plays in the planning process.

Evaluation and control

Evaluation and control are the final stages in the planning process, and are closely linked. Evaluation comprises the following activities:

1 Establishing performance targets.
2 Comparing and measuring actual performance with forecasted or budgeted targets.
3 Analysing any deviations from acceptable tolerance limits.
4 Implementing any necessary modifications.

Monitoring

Evaluation requires monitoring. Monitoring is, in effect, the measurement of progress toward the fulfilment of set objectives and of the operating budget. It also covers the situation out in the external environment, so that management can be sure that the assumptions on which the company's strategy and plans are based remain valid.

Feedback

Monitoring also involves feedback – the reporting back of relevant information and results to managers so that they can respond to any problems which occur. Thus planning can be seen as a closed loop system, with feedback on the results of plans used to update them if necessary, and to check on their progress (see Figure 3.4). Plans should never be so sacred that they cannot be changed and adapted if managers see fit.

3.5 Management by objectives (MBO)

The phrase 'management by objectives' was first used in the 1950s by Peter Drucker, who regarded it as a principle of management, co-ordinating and harmonizing the targets of the organization with those of individual managers. Drucker commented:

Management by objectives requires major effort and special instruments. For in the business enterprise managers are not automatically directed towards a common goal. On the contrary, business, by its very nature, contains three powerful factors of misdirection: in the specialized work of most managers; in the hierarchical structure of

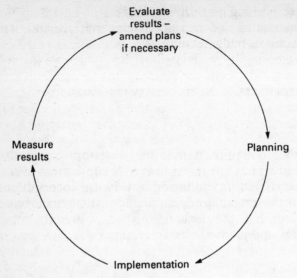

Figure 3.4   Planning loop system

management, and in the difference in vision and work and the resultant insulation of various levels of management.

Another advocate of MBO is John Humble, who sees the process as a way of integrating the need of managers to be able to contribute directly to the success of the organization and the organization's goals. Management by objectives assists the co-ordination of short-term plans with longer-term plans and goals, the co-ordination of the plans of junior and senior management, and the co-ordination of departmental plans.

The MBO process

Managers' jobs are analysed in order to determine the key areas where results are required. From these key areas, a list of key tasks the manager has to perform is drawn up. This list should be compiled jointly by the manager concerned and his superior, and normally does not consist of more than eight or nine jobs.

Short-term targets, the focus for immediate priority action by the manager, are drawn up from the key tasks. The tasks are all given a performance standard against which their attainment can be measured over a set period. The standards are either quantitative, e.g. the sales of X should be increased by 10 per cent over the coming year, or qualitative, e.g. the report on Y should be acceptable to the board. Control data for the task are normally also specified. These are sources of information against which the performance standard can be checked. In the first example above, the control data would be the relevant sales figures for the year.

At the end of the period the results of the tasks should be reviewed to assess the manager's performance. Again, this review should be conducted by both the manager's superior and the manager concerned – allowing managers to gauge how well they are doing their jobs, and realistic discussions between them and their superiors about their progress and achievements. The MBO process also allows standards and specific targets to be set for managers who are not in obviously quantifiable jobs, such as sales and production.

The advantages of MBO

1 It forces managers to think of planning for results rather than merely planning activities or work. This is important, as results-oriented planning is the only kind that makes sense.
2 It tends to force clarification of organizational roles and structures.
3 It increases commitment on a total organizational basis to the aims of the organization.
4 In addition to sparking more effective planning, MBO also assists in developing effective controls.

The disadvantages of MBO

1 A common failure of MBO is that senior management does not spend enough time teaching the philosophy of the system and selling it properly.
2 There is often failure to give adequate guidelines to those setting the objectives. Managers must know what the corporate goals are and how their tasks fit in with them.
3 A problem of MBO is that short-term targets are set,

which risks the danger of emphasizing the short term at the expense of longer-range planning.

4   Problems can arise in setting up a system that cannot adapt to rapid changes within and outside the organization. Although goals may cease to be meaningful if they are changed too often, it is nonetheless unwise to expect a manager to strive for a target that has been made obsolete by revised corporate objectives or changes in the environment.

3.6 Why planning can fail

It is evident that planning systems do sometimes fail. The reasons for their failure may be summarized as follows:

1   A lack of commitment to planning, particularly among senior managers, is often the single most important reason for failure.
2   Resistance to change.
3   Failure to see the scope of plans and the all-encompassing nature of the planning system.
4   Failure to set meaningful, verifiable objectives.
5   Over-reliance on experience; it is not always true that what happened in the past is likely to fit a future situation.
6   Poor and inflexible control techniques; planning cannot be effective unless the people responsible for it know how well it is working.
7   A hostile environment, e.g. a period of change so rapid as to require constant planning adjustments without it ever being possible to achieve identifiable results.
8   A lack of clear delegation can cause the failure of a planning system, in that it is very difficult for people to plan if they do not know what their job is and how it relates to others in the organization, and a lack of clear authority also makes it difficult to make decisions.

3.7 How planning can be effective

Planning can be effective, however, if management establishes a climate for planning. At each level of management, goals must be set, managers brought into the planning process, reviews made of subordinates' plans and performances, and checks made to ensure that people have appropriate staff assistance and information. Senior management is the single most important force in planning, and so it must be committed to the planning process. Good organization is also needed; in any business which plans effectively, planning and doing are not separated.

Importance of communication

If planning is to be effective, the goals, premises, strategies and policies have to be communicated. Perhaps the single greatest cause of unco-ordinated planning is managers' lack of understanding of their goals and of the company's strategies and policies in the area where the manager is making his decisions.

In order to establish an environment for effective planning there must be communication of these goals, policies and strategies to those who need to know them. A lack of communication can create what is known as a planning gap. In this situation the senior management understands the goals and the plans, the workers know what they have to do each day, but middle management does not understand how its departmental goals and policies tie in with those of the organization as a whole. Effective planning is fostered when managers are given the opportunity to contribute to plans which affect their areas of authority.

3.8 Summary

1 Planning can be divided into four different types and levels: corporate, strategic, management, and operational.
2 Each of these levels of planning covers a different time span and different degrees of detail and uncertainty.
3 'Management by Objectives' is one method of co-ordinating short- and long-range plans, as well as achieving measurable results, throughout the organization.
4 To have a chance of being really successful, a corporate-wide planning system has to have the active support and

backing from the senior management team, because such a system affects the entire organization and requires that everyone works towards common, well-communicated objectives and goals.

3.9 Quick questions

1   Why is planning so vital for a company?
2   How do the various types of planning differ from each other?
3   Identify the stages in the planning process.
4   What do you understand by the 'behavioural theory of the firm'?
5   Which areas of a company's business should be examined in an internal appraisal?
6   Identify the ways in which alternative strategies should be analysed and evaluated for their effects on the organization.
7   Outline the part that budgets play in planning.
8   What are the advantages of 'management by objectives'?
9   For what reasons do planning systems sometimes fail?
10   What steps can managers take to ensure that their planning is effective?

4
Organizing

This chapter looks at some of the different ways that managers can co-ordinate and arrange the work of their employees, so that all necessary tasks are completed effectively. The different organizational structures and reporting relationships are examined, as are the effects that factors like size, technology, etc., have on organizing in companies.

4.1 Organizing defined

Organizing is the part of management that co-ordinates, uses and directs whatever resources are available to the company, in order to achieve the organization's objectives. Often managers control substantial resources in terms of people, time, money, equipment, materials, and so on; and it is the first of these resources, i.e. people, which occupies much of the manager's time in his role as organizer. Urwick (1958) defined organizing from the view of an administrator: 'The purpose of organization is to secure that this division [separation and specialization of tasks] works smoothly, that there is unity of effort or, in other words, co-ordination' (Urwick, L., *The Elements of Administration*, Pitman, London).

Much of the task of organizing lies in establishing an intentional structure of roles for people in an organization to fill. It is intentional in the sense of making sure that all the tasks necessary to accomplish the objectives of the business are assigned to people competent to carry them out. Organizing therefore means determining the activities required to achieve the company's objectives; grouping these activities together into departments; assigning such groups of activities to managers; delegating the authority to carry them out; and providing for the co-ordination of all these activities, authority and information, both horizontally and vertically in the organization's structure.

4.2 Principles of organization

There are various elements (or principles) of organizational structure which tend to be common to most businesses. One set of these principles was published by Urwick in the 1940s, and subsequently revised in the early 1950s. They provide a useful starting point for discussion, and so are listed here:

1   *The principle of the objective.* Every organization and every part of the organization must be an expression of the purpose of the undertaking concerned or it is meaningless and therefore redundant.
2   *The principle of specialization.* The activities of every member of any organized group should be confined, as far as possible, to the performance of a single function.
3   *The principle of co-ordination.* The purpose of organiz-ing *per se*, as distinguished from the purpose of the undertaking, is to facilitate co-ordination; unity of effort.
4   *The principle of authority.* In every organized group the supreme authority must rest somewhere. There should be a clear line of authority from the supreme authority to every individual in the group.
5   *The principle of responsibility.* The responsibility of the superior for the acts of his subordinate is absolute.
6   *The principle of definition.* The content of each position, both the duties involved, the authority and responsibility contemplated and the relationships with other positions, should be clearly defined in writing and published to all concerned.
7   *The principle of correspondence.* In every position the responsibility and the authority should correspond.
8   *The span of control.* No person should supervise more

than five, or at the most, six, direct subordinates whose work interlocks.

9 *The principle of balance*. It is essential that the various units of an organization should be kept in balance.

10 *The principle of continuity*. Reorganization is a continuous process; in every undertaking specific provision should be made for it. (Urwick, L. *Notes on the Theory of Organization*, American Management Association, New York, 1952.)

Unity of objectives

All parts of the organization should work towards common, planned objectives. International competition and scarce resources mean that no company can afford the luxury of having parts of the organization following its own whims and not contributing to the business's goals. This is particularly true of labour-intensive organizations in the private sector, where the human resources play such a key role. People are more likely to pursue the organization's objectives rather than their own personal interests if these objectives are clearly defined and widely understood. (Unfortunately, in public sector organizations politics often lead to objectives being blurred or, worse, constantly changed, with all the consequences of loss of efficiency that that entails).

Delegation

Delegation is one of the main functions of effective management. In essence, delegation is the process which determines the expected results, assigns the tasks, confers the authority for the achievement of these tasks, and exacts responsibility for their accomplishment.

Authority and responsibility

Delegation should be a planned process if it is to be effective; the following points ought to be considered:

(*a*) Adequate authority must be given to the subordinate to carry out the task.

(b) Responsibility cannot be delegated, and therefore no superior can escape, through delegation, responsibility for the activities of his/her subordinates. At the same time, the responsibility of subordinates to their superiors for their performance is absolute, once they have accepted an assignment and the right to carry it out. It must be noted also that, since authority is the discretionary right to carry out assignments, and responsibility is the obligation to accomplish them, it follows that the authority should correspond to the responsibility. For example, if a manager gives a subordinate the authority to sell certain items, that subordinate cannot be held responsible for high rates of breakages and customer complaints caused by bad design or faulty manufacturing.

(c) The duties or responsibilities to be delegated should be clearly specified, together with a target for achievement or a timetable. Specific written delegations of authority are extremely helpful both to the manager who receives them and to the person who delegates. The latter will more easily see conflicts or overlaps with other positions, and will also be able better to identify those things for which a subordinate can and should be held responsible. Where the delegation is non-specific, managers/subordinates are forced to feel their way and to define the authority delegated to them by trial and error. In this case, unless they are familiar with top company policies and traditions, know the personality of the boss, and exercise sound judgement, they can be placed at a distinct disadvantage.

(d) Tasks should be allocated within the capability and experience of the subordinate. If the job delegated is too much for the subordinate, then the manager has not done his job responsibly and has delegated badly. An adage which is often quoted is that managers get the subordinates that they deserve (and, conversely, subordinates get the managers that they deserve). A manager who delegates badly, or who does not develop his subordinates to take responsibility and do their work well, will end up with subordinates who do their work badly and who cannot accept responsibility.

(The development and training of managers is covered later.

(*e*) Review sessions should be a regular feature in order to monitor performance and to offer constructive advice, although it must be noted that continual checking on the subordinate to assure that no mistakes are ever made will make true delegation impossible. People often learn best by the mistakes that they make, and so a subordinate must be allowed to make errors, and their cost put down as investments in that person's development.

The advantages of delegation

Whatever degree of discretion a senior manager eventually decides to give to his subordinates, the general principle is clear – senior managers should concentrate their time and effort on the major issues facing their company. Most senior managers are overworked. Delegating tasks to subordinates wherever possible is therefore good business and makes managerial sense. The tasks will then often be done more cheaply; subordinates' job satisfaction will be increased (as superiors' should be, as they will be freed from tasks which maybe are routine to them, but which still present a challenge to their subordinates); and senior managers will be more effective. It will also help develop subordinate managers for further promotion.

The 'scalar' principle

The principle that there is a vertical line of seniority/ command from the highest to the lowest level in an organization, along which authority and responsibility run from top to bottom. The more clear cut this line of authority from the most senior manager in an enterprise is to every subordinate position, the more effective will be the decision-making process, and the greater the organization's efficiency. A clear understanding of the scalar principle is necessary for the proper functioning of the organization. Subordinates must know who delegates authority down to them, and to whom matters beyond their own authority must be referred back to.

Unity of command

Unity of command is a basic management principle. The more completely an individual has a reporting relation to a single superior, the less conflict should there be in instructions, and the greater the feeling of personal responsibility for results. The larger the organization, however, the more difficult it is to observe this 'unity of command'. Some organizational structures moreover do deliberately flout this principle, e.g. matrix structure. This does create some problems, but under certain circumstances these problems are outweighed by the advantages the types of structure also bring.

The span of control

The span of control concerns the number of subordinates reporting directly to a supervisor. There are many different numbers suggested as the most that a manager should have reporting to him. Urwick's limit is five or six, if their work interlocks. If their work does not interlock, then one manager can supervise more subordinates, but the highest theoretical figure put forward is eight or nine only.

Determining the span of control

The appropriate span of control does depend on a variety of factors. These include:

1 Whether the subordinates are qualified to make decisions without having constantly to refer upwards to the manager. If they are, the number reporting to the manager can be increased.
2 Whether the manager is prepared to delegate authority to subordinates; if not, then the number of subordinates will not be large.
3 A manager can supervise more people if the organization has a well defined planning function and an agreed set of objectives.
4 If an organization has a developed, tried and tested communication system that feeds information quickly to

and from senior management, each manager is able to control a large number of people.

5 Some organizations, particularly those in the public sector, depend a great deal on personal contact to operate effectively. These types of organization will inevitably have small spans of control and many levels of subordinates and co-ordinators.

The effect of different degrees of sophistication of technology on spans of control was shown by Joan Woodward in a study of 100 manufacturing companies (*Industrial Organization: Theory and Practice* OUP, London, 1965). The median span of control of the chief executives in firms using unit production processes was four, that in mass-production companies seven, and in process production firms ten. The number of people the first-line supervisors controlled also varied greatly, depending on the production process used: the average number in unit production firms was twenty-three, in mass production/large batch firms forty-nine, and in process production companies thirteen.

4.3 Types of organizational structure

Structure has been defined as 'the established pattern of relationships among the parts of the organization'. There are two types of organizational structure which exist side by side: a formal structure and an informal one.

The formal organization

This is the organization designed by senior management in order to achieve the objectives of the organization, and to promote efficiency and effectiveness. Thus the design of the formal organization is guided by the principles of unity of objective (which has already been noted) and of efficiency. The principle of efficiency holds that an organization's structure is efficient if it helps people accomplish the company's objectives with the minimum unforeseen consequences and costs, i.e. if it promotes good management. At the same time, however, there should be room for discretion, for taking advantage of the creative talents and for the recognition of individual likes and capacities, in the most formal of organizations.

It must be noted that there is nothing inherently inflexible about formal structures of organization. On the contrary, if the manager is to organize well, structure must furnish an environment in which individual performance, both present and future, contributes to the group goals.

The informal organization

Within every organization, alongside the formal organizational structure, there exists the informal structure. This is based on relations between individuals and groups, and as such is much more dynamic and less easily definable than the more rigid, formal structure.

In many ways, these informal structures, because they reflect the present, real world situation rather than what managers think the situation is, are more powerful than the formal organizational links. If the two situations seriously diverge, it may become necessary to formalize at least some of the informal relations; otherwise communication channels may break down and managers' freedom of action be curtailed.

4.4 Centralization or decentralization?

All companies have to decide just what degree of decentralized power they will have in their structure. The inevitable push towards specialization in all but the smallest of organizations leads to the diffusion of authority and accountability. The need to structure activities develops logically into the need to allocate appropriate amounts of authority to those responsible for undertaking those activities. Every organization of any size must therefore consider how much authority to delegate from the centre.

The concept of centralization can be used in a number of ways. It can be understood in terms of performance and also in geographical terms. But when centralization is discussed as an aspect of management, it refers to withholding or delegating authority for decision-making. A highly centralized organization is one where little authority (and especially over major areas of the business) is exercised outside a key group of senior managers. On the other hand, a highly decentralized company is one in which the authority to organize men, money and materials is widely diffused throughout every level of the structure.

The case for centralization

Centralization has a number of advantages:

1 Support services can be provided more cheaply on a company-wide, rather than on a departmental basis.
2 The company often can employ a higher calibre of staff.
3 Tight control can be maintained over the company's cashflow and expenditure.

The case for decentralization

The advantages of decentralization are as follows:

1 It prevents top management overload by freeing it from many day-to-day operational decisions, enabling top managers to concentrate on their more important strategic responsibilities.
2 It enables local management to be flexible in its approach to decisions in the light of local conditions, and thus be more adaptable in situations of rapid change.
3 It speeds up operational decisions by enabling line managers to take local action without referring back to their superiors all the time.
4 It focuses attention on to important cost and profit centres within the organization, sharpening management awareness of the importance of cost-effectiveness, as well as revenue targets.
5 It can contribute to staff motivation by enabling middle and junior managers to get a taste of real responsibility, and by generally encouraging initiative by all employees.

On balance, most companies opt for at least a certain amount of decentralization, principally because of the enormous pressures on modern business organizations to concede more and more authority to staff at executive and specialist levels. However, it should not be thought that this is a static principle: the amount of decentralization that occurs should vary as the circumstances of the company vary, to meet the needs of the situation at the time. For example, a merger between two companies might promote a greater degree of centralization for a while, especially if one company is experiencing financial trouble (prompting the merger). The quality of the business's middle management will also determine the amount and differing pace of decentralization – if they are good, the senior managers are liable to delegate more and decentralize authority more.

4.5 Departmentation

Every organization has to carry out certain activities in order to accomplish its goals. The senior manager therefore has to decide how to group together the various activities and individuals within the organization. This is known as 'departmentation', which simply means the process of splitting the business into departments. The main forms of departmentation are as follows:

1 *By geographical area* – it is obviously useful where it is important to be close to the territory in which the organization wants to operate. For example, a company based in Britain may consider that its market is the whole of Western Europe. Rather than attempting to do anything from its head office, it may divide up the sales function (and later the production function), placing a separate operation in each country.

2 *By function* – here activities are grouped around business functions such as production, marketing and finance. Occasionally organizations also have departments built around managerial functions such as planning and controlling. Functional departmentation has an important advantage in that it is a logical and time-proven method. It is also the best way of making certain that the power and prestige of the basic activities of the enterprise will be defended by top managers. Another advantage is that functional departmentation follows the principle of occupational specialization, so assisting the efficient utiliza-

tion of people. It must be noted, however, that the more numerous and specialized the various departments are, the more difficult the task of senior management to co-ordinate and to manage becomes.

3 *By product* – as organizations grow, so the range of products they offer grows. At first, all goods and services are handled by means of common facilities, but there comes a time when the volume being dealt with is so large that advantages are to be gained by treating each product as a separate company. Product is an important basis for departmentation, because it helps the organization make the best use of economies of scale and specialized knowledge, as well as personal skills.

4 *By customer* – this form of departmentation is particularly common in the sales function, where it is felt that different kinds of customers require different treatment. This is so particularly in the food manufacturing industry, where a distinction is made between the small independent shop and the large multiple supermarket chain.

5 *By process or equipment* – the grouping of activities about a process or a type of equipment is often employed by manufacturing companies. A good example of equipment departmentation is the existence of electronic data-processing departments. The purpose of such departmentation is to achieve economic advantages, although it may also be required by the nature of the equipment.

6 *By time* – organizing according to time-scales, e.g. day and night shifts, makes sense where round-the-clock production is used, and where over long periods the human response is limited in its operational capability.

7 *By numbers* – the numbers method of departmentation is achieved by tolling off persons who are to perform the same duties and putting them under a manager. The essential fact is not what these people do or where they work, but that the success of the undertaking depends only upon the number of people.

4.6 Organizational relationships

Whatever span of control is chosen, whatever the number and arrangement of departments eventually decided upon, the company's management then has the choice of various tried and tested organizational relationships within the structure finally decided upon.

Line relationships

First there are line relationships operating within an organization. These are the direct working relationships between the vertical levels of the organizational structure, i.e. it is the authority that every manager exercises in respect of his own subordinates. This is the most common type of organizational and working relationship. It has the advantages that formal communication channels are clear, authority and responsibility are agreed upon, and instructions and information flow up and down between the individuals concerned. Line authority is the central feature of the total chain of command throughout the entire organization.

Staff relationships

Staff relationships also operate within the organization. The nature of the staff relationship is advisory. The function of people in a purely staff capacity (such as personnel, finance, IT and administration) is to investigate, research, and give advice to the company's line managers. It is important to be able to make a distinction between line and staff relationships. Both manager and subordinate alike must know whether they are acting in a staff or line capacity. If they act in a staff capacity, their job is merely to advise their line manager colleagues: not to order or command. It is up to the line managers to make the decisions and issue instructions.

It must be noted, however, that in many organizations the difference between the line and staff function is not so clear cut. In such companies one often finds staff manager specialists who also have line responsibility over their own subordinates. For example, the personnel manager will have a staff relationship to the managing director on personnel policy, but line responsibility over employees in the training, employment, recruitment and safety sections of his own personnel department. See Figure 4.1.

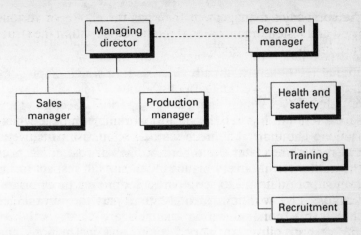

Figure 4.1 Line and staff relationships

Functional relationships

A third type of relationship operating within an organization is the functional relationship. Functional authority is the right which an individual or department may have delegated to them to control specific processes, policies, or other matters throughout the company, by virtue of their specialist knowledge or function. So, for example, a company's finance director is not only responsible for the conduct of financial matters, but also has the authority to insist that line managers should adhere to the company's established financial procedures and policies. It must be noted that functional authority is not restricted to managers of a particular type of department; it may be exercised by line or staff department heads.

Committee relationships

Committee relationships also play an important part in organizational structures. Committees can either be formal, i.e. have a written remit and the authority to carry out a specific function, or informal, set up for some temporary purpose, e.g. to act as a pressure valve or as a sounding board for management.

Matrix relationships

Finally there are what are known as matrix relationships. A matrix relationship is a combination of the other organizational relationships already discussed, in which employees and managers have dual responsibilities. First, they have a responsibility to their immediate superiors. Second, they have a relationship to the specialist working groups of which they are members. The main featue of a matrix structure is that it combines lateral and vertical lines of communication and authority. Matrix relationships can be set up for a limited period only – to see a particular project through, for example – or as a permanent, normal part of the organizational structure.

Matrix structures are very flexible, and can help a company adapt quickly to changes in its environment. They do have their disadvantages, however:

1 Potential conflicts can arise about the allocation of resources and the division of authority between project groups and functional specialists, leading to the dilution of function management responsibilities throughout the organization.
2 There is also the possibility of a division of loyalty on the part of members of project teams in relation to their project managers and their functional superiors, because the teams have to report to two bosses.

Despite these disadvantages, the matrix organizational structure probably offers the best answer to date to the problem of handling the tension between, on the one hand, the need to differentiate, and, on the other, the need to integrate, the complex activities of the modern company. Any difficulties which do occur with such a relationship are probably best resolved in a less rigid organization, where most problems can be sorted out by informal, quick discussions.

4.7 Organizational problems for managers

Organizing the resources under their control is one of the most difficult functions managers have to undertake and, whatever the solutions and structures ultimately chosen, most managers will encounter a number of problems. The first of these often arises out of imprecise, unachievable objectives, which do not have the commitment of the employees concerned. Failings regarding delegation and vagueness of working relationships also create problems for the manager, as well as lack of feedback, inadequate communication systems, and breakdowns in the chain of command, such as the mixing up of line and staff relationships.

4.8 Summary

1 Organizing comprises determining the physical framework or structure of the company to allow staff to work most effectively and efficiently.
2 This organizational structure is affected by such factors as the firm's size, the technology it uses, its objectives and goals, and so on.
3 Because of this, and because these factors change over time, there is no one best structure for an organization. The structure chosen should be appropriate for that time, but it should also be flexible enough to adapt to changing circumstances.

4.9 Quick questions

1 What does the organizing process involve for managers?
2 Identify Urwick's principles of organization.
3 What factors should be taken into account when the delegation of work is being considered?
4 How does an organization's size and technology affect its span of control?
5 Compare the advantages and disadvantages of formal and informal structures of organization.
6 What factors lead companies to adopt greater or lesser degrees of decentralization?
7 List the main forms of departmentation.
8 What are the sorts of structural relationships that may exist in companies?

5
Leading and leadership

The manager's role of leader is looked at in this chapter, which covers the importance of providing good leadership and guidance in organizations, different theories about the nature of leadership, and the various leadership styles which can be found in companies.

5.1 Introduction

There are various definitions of leadership. Drucker defines general leadership as 'The lifting of a man's vision to higher sights, the raising of man's performance to a higher standard, the building of man's personality beyond its normal limitations'.

Managerial leadership can be defined, in more prosaic terms, as the process of directing and influencing the work of team members. Leading is concerned with guiding and directing others. Leaders/managers act to help a group attain its objectives with the maximum application of its capabilities. They do not stand behind the group to push it in a certain direction; they place themselves in front of it to facilitate progress and inspire the group to accomplish organizational goals.

It must be noted that, although at times the terms 'leader' and 'manager' are treated as synonymous, there does need to be a distinction between leadership and management. *Leadership* is the ability to shape the attitudes and behaviour of others. *Management* is the formal task of decision and command. Leadership is one important aspect of a manager's job, but it is not all of it.

5.2 The importance of leadership

In *The Practice of Management* Drucker cautions against organizations relying upon leadership, instead of good management, as, although leadership is very important, it is also a rare commodity:

> Leadership is of utmost importance. Indeed there is no substitute for it . . . but it cannot be taught or learned . . . There is no substitute for leadership. But management cannot create leaders. It can only create the conditions under which potential leadership qualities become effective; or it can stifle potential leadership. The supply of leadership is much too limited and unpredictable to be depended upon for the creation of the spirit the business enterprise needs to be productive and to hold together. Management must work on creating the spirit by other means. These means may be less effective and more pedestrian. But at least they are available and within management's control. In fact, to concentrate on leadership may only too easily lead management to do nothing at all about the spirit of the organization.

Certainly, however, leadership can be identified as an important element of effective management. The functions of management undertaken by the manager will produce far greater results if they have added to them the ingredient of effective leadership. When this effective leadership permeates the whole enterprise, the result is a successful organization.

5.3 Leadership theories

Three theories of leadership will be looked at here – the personality or behavioural approach, the situational approach, and the contingency theory of leadership.

Personality traits

The earliest studies of leadership were based largely on an attempt to identify the traits that leaders actually possessed.

In searching for measurable leadership traits, researchers took two approaches:

1   Comparison of the traits of leaders and non-leaders. This is the most common approach, but it has failed to reveal any traits that consistently set leaders apart from followers. As a group, leaders have been found to be taller, brighter, more extrovert and self-confident than non-leaders. However, many people have these traits and do not achieve a leadership position, while many people acknowledged as leaders do not possess these traits (both Alexander the Great and Napoleon were of below average height, for example). Psychologist E. E. Jennings perhaps understood the real value of this approach when he wrote: 'Fifty years of study have failed to produce one personality trait or set of qualities that can be used to discriminate between leaders and non-leaders'.
2   Comparison of the traits of effective leaders with those of ineffective leaders. Studies which have taken this approach have also failed to isolate traits that are strongly associated with successful leadership.

Situational approach

It was because of the inconclusiveness of the studies into the personality traits of leaders that the situational theory of leadership developed. According to this, people follow those leaders who they think are best placed to enable them to achieve their own personal goals and objectives.

Fiedler's contingency approach to leadership

According to Fiedler, people become leaders not only because of the attributes of their personality but also because of the interaction between them and changing situations. Therefore, an effective leader is one who can lead in all situations.

Action-centred leadership

John Adair developed the idea of action-centred, or functional leadership. According to him there are three variables in the work situation: task needs, group needs and individual needs. The effective leader has to balance each of these needs against the demands of the total situation at that point in time. The leader has to judge which should have priority and at what time. This approach to leadership is very flexible and depends entirely upon the circumstances of the situation. The three sets of needs are interconnected, as is shown in Figure 5.1.

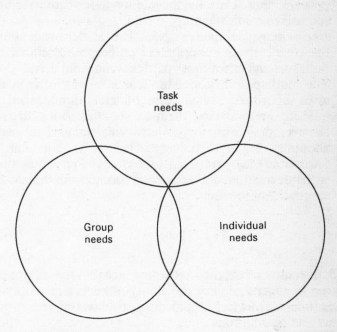

Figure 5.1   Needs at work

This interconnection means that actions taken in relation to one particular set of needs will have an effect upon the other two. For example, if the leader concentrates on building up group motivation, his action is liable to motivate the individuals making up the group as well, and the effect of both is usually the accomplishment of the task in hand. Conversely, if the leader neglects one section of needs, the needs of the other two will not be met fully either – if task needs are ignored, then the group will cease to have goals to aim at and the individuals will have no occupation or purpose.

5.4 Leadership styles

Some earlier explanations of leadership styles classified them on the basis of how leaders use their authority. These regard managers as applying three basic styles, as follows:

1 *Autocratic style*. The autocratic leader is seen as one who commands and expects compliance, who is dogmatic and positive, and leads by the ability to give or withhold rewards or punishment.
2 *Democratic/participative style*. The leader who adopts this style consults subordinates on proposed actions and decisions and encourages participation from them.
3 The third style of leadership is one in which the leader gives subordinates a substantial degree of independence in their work, leaving them to set their own goals and discover their own way of achieving them. The leader adopting this style perceives his/her role as one of facilitating the operations of followers by providing them with information, and acting as a contact with the group's external environment.

McGregor's theory X and theory Y

The style adopted, whether autocratic or more participative, will depend in part upon the manager's view of human nature in general, and of the ability of his/her subordinates in particular. McGregor laid down two sets of contrasting views and assumptions.

Theory X

1 'The average human being has an inherent dislike of work and will avoid it if he can.
2 'Because of this human characteristic of dislike of work, most people must be coerced, controlled, directed [or] threatened with punishment to get them to put forth adequate effort toward the achievement of organizational objectives.
3 'The average human being prefers to be directed, wishes to avoid responsibility, has relatively little ambition, [and] wants security above all.'

Theory X managers will favour autocratic or perhaps paternalistic management styles.

Theory Y

1 'The expenditure of physical and mental effort in work
   is as natural as play or rest. The average human being
   does not inherently dislike work. Depending upon the
   controllable conditions, work may be a source of satisfaction or a source of punishment.
2 'External control and the threat of punishment are not
   the only means for bringing about effort toward organizational objectives. Man will exercise self-direction and
   self-control in the service of objectives to which he is
   committed.
3 'Commitment to objectives is a [result] of the rewards
   associated with their achievement . . .
4 'The average human being learns, under proper conditions not only to accept but to seek responsibility . . .
5 'The capacity to exercise a relatively high degree of
   imagination, ingenuity and creativity in the solution of
   organizational problems is widely, not narrowly, distributed in the population.
6 'Under conditions of modern industrial life, the intellec-
   tual potentialities of the average human being are only
   partially utilized.'

This Theory Y encourages a more participative style of
management, or at least consultative leadership rather than
leadership by the imposition of decisions.

Likert's styles of management leadership

Likert has identified four styles or systems of management:
exploitative–authoritative, benevolent–authoritative, consultative, and participative–group.

1 *Exploitative–authoritative*. Managers who adopt this style
  are highly autocratic, place little trust in subordinates
  and use fear and punishment as motivators, with only

occasional rewards. They retain all powers of decision-making and only engage in downward communication.

2   *Benevolent–authoritative*. Managers of this style are paternalistic, placing a condescending trust and confidence in subordinates, whom they motivate with rewards and some punishment. They allow some upward communication and opinions from lower levels and also allow some delegation of decision-making, though with close policy control.

3   *Consultative*. Managers adopting this style of management seek out the opinions and ideas of subordinates and work to put them to constructive use. The consultative style is also evident in their engaging in communication upwards and downwards and encouraging some participation in decision-making.

4   *Participative–group*. Managers adopting this style show complete confidence and trust in subordinates in all matters. They use the ideas and opinions of subordinates and motivate them through economic rewards and participation, and involvement in setting goals and undertaking appraisal of these goals. In effect, these managers operate as part of a group consisting of both peers and subordinates.

It is this last style of management leadership which Likert regards as the most effective. Its effectiveness arises out of the group/unit concept it operates upon. All members of the group, including the manager or leader, adopt a supportive relationship in which they feel a genuine common interest, in terms of needs, values, aspirations, goals and expectations.

Managerial grid – Blake and Mouton

Blake and Mouton's managerial grid (Figure 5.2) is a two-dimensional measurement of managers' leadership style. One axis of the grid represents production, and the other represents the human element in businesses – people. Scores are allocated from 1 to 10 along both axes (1 = low, 10 = high). Using this grid, Blake and Mouton identified four extreme styles of management:

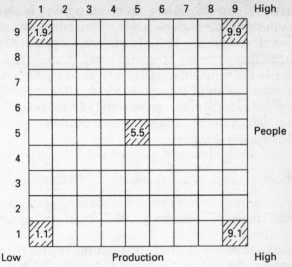

Figure 5.2 Managerial grid

1 *Impoverished management.* This style of management reflects low scores on both axes, as managers show little concern for either people or production. They seem to have little idea of the requirements of management.
2 The antithesis of impoverished management occurs when managers are dedicated both to production and people, scoring high on both axes.
3 *Country club management.* Here the manager scores low on the production scale and has little concern for production. Rather, he is concerned primarily for people in his role as manager, and places great emphasis on promoting a relaxed and friendly environment. The creation of such a working environment is made at the expense of any co-ordinated effort to accomplish organizational goals.
4 *Autocratic task managers.* These managers score highly on the production scale but low on the people scale. They are concerned only with developing an efficient operation and have little or no concern for people. They are quite autocratic in their style of leadership.

Reddin – 3–D theory of management effectiveness

The managerial grid of Blake and Mouton above suffers from being only a two-dimensional measurement of management style. It does not take into account that the four basic managerial styles can all be more or less effective, depending upon the particular circumstances the styles are used in. The style that is most effective some of the time is not necessarily the most effective all of the time. Therefore, to the two dimensions of Blake and Mouton's grid, Reddin has added a third, measuring 'managerial effectiveness' – or the extent to which the management style used meets the needs of the particular situation.

A contingency approach to leadership effectiveness

The effectiveness of a manager's leadership style, according to Fiedler, depends upon three critical situational dimensions:

1 *Positional power*. In this situation the leader derives the power necessary to get group members to comply with directions from his position within the organizational structure of authority, rather than from personal charisma or expertise.
2 *Task structure*. The extent to which tasks are clearly and specifically spelled out and individuals can be held responsible for their execution.
3 *Leader–member relations*. The extent to which group members like and trust the leader and are willing to follow his directions.

These variables alter, and so the manager has to change his style of approach in order to fit the changes in circumstances.

The Vroom–Yetton leadership model

Yetton and Vroom developed a model to show which out of five management styles (ranging from autocratic to group decision-making) could be used effectively in dealing with different situations. Their work demonstrates that in practice managers do not usually just use one leadership approach or style, but respond and adapt to circumstances: 'Whereas once there were only participative or autocratic managers, we now find that it makes as much sense to talk about participative and autocratic problems' (Yetton and Vroom, 1978).
    The five management styles are:

A1 The manager solves the problem or makes a decision on the information he has available at the time.

A11 The manager gets any information he needs from subordinates, and then makes a decision. The subordinates supply specific information in answer to the manager's requests; they do not define or discuss the problem at all.

C1 The manager asks the views of individual subordinates, and then makes his decision.

C11 The manager asks the views of his subordinates in a group meeting, and then makes his decision.

G11 The manager shares the problem with his subordinates as a group, and tries to reach a consensus decision. The manager's role here is really that of chairman.

Vroom and Yetton then define seven situational variables, in the form of questions, which should be used with the leadership model. These are:

1 Does the problem possess a quality requirement?
2 Do I have sufficient information to make a high-quality decision?
3 Is the problem structured?
4 Is the acceptance of the decision by my subordinates important for its effective implementation?
5 If I were to make the decision by myself, am I reasonably certain that it would be accepted by my subordinates?
6 Do my subordinates share the organizational goals to be attained in solving this problem?
7 Is conflict among my subordinates likely with the preferred solution?

The leadership model, showing (in the form of a decision tree) the set of managerial styles which could be used in response to the questions/variables given, is shown in Figure 5.3.

5.5 Summary

1 Leadership is a very important aspect of a manager's job. A manager who is a good leader will achieve better results

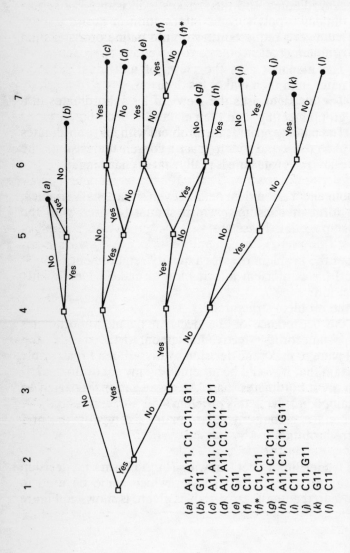

(a) A1, A11, C1, C11, G11
(b) G11
(c) A1, A11, C1, C11, G11
(d) A1, A11, C1, C11
(e) G11
(f) C11
(f)* C1, C11
(g) A11, C1, C11
(h) A11, C1, C11, G11
(i) C11
(j) C11, G11
(k) G11
(l) C11

Figure 5.3 Vroom–Yetton leadership model

Source: Yetton, P. W. and Vroom, V. H. (1978) 'The Vroom–Yetton model of leadership, an overview', in *Managerial Control and Organizational Democracy* (eds King, Strenfert and Fiedler)

than one who is a poor leader, by organizing and guiding the people working for him, and by enabling them to do their jobs well.
2 The way in which this can be done will vary according to the particular needs of the situation. Sometimes a manager may need to use a more autocratic approach than normal, and at other times a participative approach.

5.6 Quick questions

1 How can managerial leadership be defined?
2 Explain the 'contingency approach' to leadership.
3 What is 'action-centred' or 'functional' leadership?
4 Differentiate between Theory X managers and Theory Y managers.
5 List Rensis Likert's management styles.
6 According to Fiedler, what are the three critical variables which determine the effectiveness of a particular management style?

5.7 Exercise

Using Blake and Mouton's managerial grid, consider the management style of:

(i) your company in general (or an organization you are familiar with) – this will depend upon the organization's business ethos, and upon the chief executive's style and personality;
(ii) your superior (if applicable)
(iii) yourself.

Bearing in mind the drawbacks of this two-dimensional grid, are there any improvements in the styles you have identified that you can suggest?

6
Motivating

Some of the problems managers face in trying to motivate their subordinates and staff are looked at in this chapter. Various motivation theories, from those concentrating on job content to process and contingency theories are discussed, as are some of the ways of motivating employees.

6.1 Introduction

Motivation may be defined as the total propensity or level of desire of an individual to behave in a certain manner at a certain time. Within the context of the organization, motivation can be defined as the willingness of an individual to respond to organizational requirements in the short run.

A motivated person is said to have latent energy, which is *potentially* available for an effective performance. But this general state of being does not guarantee that the individual will behave appropriately in a given situation. The motivation within has to be directed toward a specific goal; it then becomes what is known as a 'motive for behaviour'.

Choices and priorities

Unfortunately, motivation is not quite so simple as that. It causes persons to make choices, from the available alternatives, about how to best allocate their energy and time. Most people are engaged in many activities and with several groups, creating a multitude of relationships, and as the individual does not have unlimited time or energy, he/she must choose on which activities to expend both. People tend to be more motivated in activities/relationships that offer the greatest perceived rewards or the fewest penalties, i.e. they will observe priorities.

It is important that both the organization and managers understand this when they try to motivate employees, for from this it can be said that individuals who are not performing effectively within the organization are not necessarily lacking in motivation. Rather, they may not have been motivated in such a way as to give their role within the organization priority over other relationships and situations. Thus managers often do not merely have to motivate their subordinates, but motivate them in the right direction.

6.2 Motivation and personality

Motivation cannot be accomplished in a vacuum independent of the individual's 'needs', 'wants' and 'fears'. The central problem of motivation therefore, as far as the manager is concerned, is how to induce a group of people with different needs, wants, fears and personalities to work together, towards the objectives of the organization. The part these needs, wants, and fears play in motivating people has been recognized by the human relations school of management theory, in particular by Abraham Maslow, whose theory of human motivation will be discussed later on.

Needs and perceptions

Needs and perceptions are the bases on which an individual's level of motivation are established. Needs may be defined as desired but as yet unrealized values; and perceptions as organized impressions of one's place in a particular environment, both as to the present and the anticipated future.

6.3 Theories of motivation

Motivation theories can be divided into two types: content theories and process theories. According to content motivation theories, which are looked at first, individuals are motivated by a 'package' of needs and wants which they pursue. Maslow's hierarchy of needs, and Herzberg's two-factor motivation theory are examples of content theories.

Process theories of motivation, however, examine the way in which certain outcomes of events become attractive to people, and therefore are pursued by them. Process theories include Handy's motivation calculus and Vroom's expectancy theory. These are different from content theories, because they assume that individuals can choose their own needs and goals.

Management theories and motivation

The classical school of management assumes that workers are self-seeking, and only motivated by pay; and so maximum efficiency can be achieved by assembly-line manufacturing processes for high rates of pay. However, breaking down jobs into their most simple elements, so that a day's work on, say, a car assembly line consists of repeating a task which has to be completed in under a minute several thousand times, creates mind-numbingly tedious jobs. Motivation will always be a problem in such industries, regardless of how much the employees are paid, and it tends to show itself in high staff-turnover rates, high absenteeism, and generally low morale.

The research of Elton Mayo in the early 1930s into productivity at the Western Electric Company showed conclusively that workers were definitely not just motivated by economic motives, but that social contact and work-group self-government were powerful motivators.

Maslow's theory of human motivation

Abraham Maslow advanced a number of important propositions about human behaviour. First, he recognized that humans are wanting creatures, i.e. they want things, and continually want more. Even though specific needs can become satiated, needs in general do not. Second, Maslow proposed that a satisfied need does not act as a motivator; only unsatisfied needs motivate behaviour. Third, human needs are arranged in a series of levels – a hierarchy of

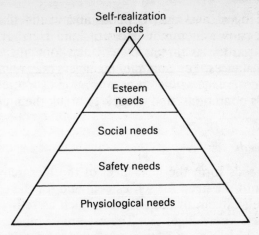

Figure 6.1 Maslow's hierarchy of needs (1954)

importance. As soon as needs on a lower level are fulfilled, those on the next level will emerge and demand satisfaction.

Physiological needs

At the lowest level are physiological needs. These are needs which must be satisfied to maintain life. They include the need for food, water, air, etc. Until these are satisfied, they act as the primary motivators, taking precedence over any other needs. Thus a starving person will not be motivated by desires for self-fulfilment, but by the need to obtain food.

Safety needs

The next level up the hierarchy is that of safety needs. These come into operation as effective motivators only after a person's physiological needs have been reasonably satisfied. These needs take the form of the desire for protection from physical danger, economic security, an orderly and predictable world, etc.

Social needs

The third level is that of social needs. Once again these only become effective motivators as needs for safety become reasonably satisfied. They include the need to belong, to be accepted, to give and receive friendship and affection. Social needs act as powerful motivators of human behaviour but may be regarded as threats by organizations' management in some instances. For example, managers may regard some informal groupings within an organization as a threat to the company's operations, and so seek to break them up.

Esteem needs

Esteem needs form the next level of the hierarchy. These include both the need for self-esteem and for the esteem of others. Self-esteem includes aspects such as self-confience, self-respect, knowledge, etc. The esteem of others includes the need for their respect, recognition, appreciation, and for status in their eyes. The competitive desire to excel is an almost universal trait. This is a major esteem need, and if properly harnessed by management can produce extremely high organizational performance. A manager's stimulation of these needs can bring feelings of worth and value, but if they are unfulfilled, feelings of inferiority, helplessness and weakness arise. It must be noted, however, that, unlike the lower levels of needs, esteem needs are rarely completely satisfied, and tend to be insatiable.

Self-realization needs

At the pinnacle of Maslow's hierarchy of needs is the need for self-realization. This is individuals' need for realizing their own potential, for self-fulfilment and continued self-development, for being creative in the broadest sense of the term. The specific form of these needs will vary from one individual to another.

Money as a need

Maslow does not include pay or money specifically as a need in his hierarchy. He considered money as a means of satisfying various other needs at the different levels. Money is of course most important in satisfying lower levels of needs in the hierarchy.

Qualifications of Maslow's theory

Maslow's theory, which we have just outlined, can be applied generally but not specifically. It is dynamic rather than static. In addition, it must be recognized that levels in the hierarchy are not rigidly fixed but do tend to overlap. Another qualification of the theory is that the chain of causation may not always run from stimulus to individual needs to behaviour. Although the theory states that a person deprived of two needs will want the more basic of them, they may not act this out logically, as other factors may influence them. Further problems associated with Maslow's theory are that the same need will not lead to the same response in all individuals, who may develop substitute goals if direct achievement of a need is blocked; and many of the things which humans strive for are remote, long-range goals that can be achieved only in a series of steps.

Herzberg's two-factor theory (1966)

Herzberg has provided an alternative explanation of the ways in which factors such as salary, achievement, and working conditions affect the motivation to work. He asked 200 engineers and accountants about the factors which improved or reduced their job satisfaction. Two distinct groups of factors were identified, as in Table 6.1.

Table 6.1   Factors in job motivation

Hygiene factors	Motivators
Company policy	Achievement
Salary	Recognition
Supervision	Responsibility
Working conditions	Job itself

Hygiene factors

These factors created a favourable environment for motivation and prevented job dissatisfaction. They included company policy and administration, supervision, salary, interpersonal relations and working conditions. If any of these areas were found to be sub-standard or poor, there tended to be job dissatisfaction. But the presence of good levels of hygiene factors do not in themselves create job satisfaction.

Motivators

Motivators promote job satisfaction when they are present, but only when hygiene factors are present at satisfactory levels. Motivators include achievement, recognition, the work itself, responsibility and advancement. The common element in these motivators is that they are all related to the intrinsic nature of the work itself; they are not merely elements or circumstances surrounding the job.

Thus, satisfaction and dissatisfaction are not simple opposites; each is governed by its own group of factors – satisfaction by motivators and dissatisfaction by hygiene factors. To remove causes of dissatisfaction is not the same as creating satisfaction.

Maslow and Herzberg

There is a strong similarity between Maslow's hierarchy of needs and Herzberg's classification of factors influencing motivation and job satisfaction or dissatisfaction. Hygiene factors correspond to Maslow's basic physiological, safety, and social needs; whereas motivators correspond to the higher growth needs in the hierarchy. See Table 6.2.

Table 6.2   Similarity between theories of Maslow and Herzberg

Maslow	Herzberg
Self-realisation Esteem needs	Motivating factors
Social needs Safety needs Physiological needs	Hygiene factors

Herzberg's analysis, if it is correct, has important implications for personnel management. For example, the provision of welfare services may improve the working environment, but will not motivate people to work.

McClelland – motivating needs

David McClelland identified three basic motivating needs which, to some extent, correspond to Maslow's social, esteem and self-realization needs. McClelland measured the levels of these needs in various individuals, discovering that the existence of one need did not preclude the existence of the others, and an individual may be strongly motivated by a combination of all three.

The three motivating needs which McClelland identified were the following:

1 *The need for affiliation*. People with a strong need for affiliation usually derive pleasure from a group they enjoy intimacy, understanding and friendly interaction with, and are concerned with maintaining good relationships.
2 *The need for power*. Those with a strong need for power want to exercise influence and control. They seek positions of leadership, and tend to be argumentative, demanding, forceful, and good communicators.
3 *The need for achievement*. People with a strong need for achievement have an intense desire for success and an equally intense fear of failure.

Further research by McClelland revealed that managers as a whole had strong needs for achievement and power, but low affiliation needs. Although those who have strong achievement needs tend to advance faster than others, it must be noted that managing requires other characteristics besides a drive for success and achievement. A need for affiliation is important too, as managers have to work and get on well with other people, and to co-ordinate their efforts within the organization.

6.4 Process theories of motivation

As was explained earlier, Herzberg, Maslow and McClelland's theories of motivation are content theories. We shall now examine some of the more recent process theories of motivation.

Equity theory – Adams

Adams maintains that the absolute situations of workers are less important than people's situations *in comparison* to other similar workers or to what the people feel their situations ought to be. Any perceived inequalities, e.g. in wage levels, tend to create unease and dissatisfaction, and therefore will affect the individual's motivation to work.

Two important points should be noted: first, that the situation of the worker may not actually be unfair, but just *seems* to be unfair; second, unease will occur if the inequality works in the individual's favour, as well as if the person thinks he/she is getting a bad deal. If people do not think that they are being adequately rewarded (either by money or recognition) for the effort they put into a job, they will reduce that effort to a level which they think is appropriate for the rewards they receive.

Expectancy theory – Vroom

The level of motivation a person feels for doing a particular activity depends upon the extent to which the results are expected to contribute to his/her own particular needs and goals.

Motivation calculus

Following on from this expectancy theory, it can be said that the strength of individuals' motivation is a factor of the strength of their preference for the particular outcome, and the expectation that this outcome will occur if certain behaviour is used or actions carried out. Usually this calculation is not consciously made each time a person decides to do something. But certainly, for major decisions, such as whether or not to change jobs, most people do at least consider the points for and against a move.

Contingency approach to motivation

Theorists such as Kurt Levin point out that an individual's motivation cannot be looked at in isolation, because people interact with life outside the organization, and with others inside it as well. So persons' motivation depends upon more than just their needs and expectations, and will change according to circumstances. Being complex, even fickle creatures, different people react in different ways to things, and an individual's level of motivation can change from day to day, depending on how he/she feels.

6.5 Ways of motivating staff

Chris Argyris maintains that the work situation of an individual will affect the personal development and potential of that person. He identifies seven stages of development from infant to mature behaviour:

Infant passivity	– Adult activity
Dependence	– Independence
Limited behaviours	– Many different behaviours
Erratic and brief interests	– Stable deeper interests
Short time perspective	– Longer time perspective
Subordinate social position	– Equal/superior position
Lack of self-awareness	– Self-awareness and self-control

Argyris' contention is that many organizations do not encourage their staff to develop into mature patterns of behaviour in their work: jobs are reduced to minimal routine tasks, wider thinking is discouraged, and most staff take no part in making decisions. In other words, the organizations are promoting and encouraging McGregor's Theory X management.

In contrast, Argyris would like to see companies practising Theory Y management: encouraging greater participation by their employees, better communications, and job enlargement and enrichment, so that people have the opportunity to develop as individuals. This would benefit both the employees and the organization.

Job enrichment, defined by Herzberg as 'the planned process of up-grading the responsibility, challenge, and content of the work' can definitely increase persons' motivation, as it tends to give them more power over decisions which affect them, and generally adds to the interest and responsibility of the job – although the extra responsibility of the work has to be appropriately rewarded.

Job enlargement increases the number of operations one person does in one task cycle. This is more of a hygiene factor, because it should help to reduce the repetition and boredom of the work, although it is unlikely to increase motivation among the workforce.

Unfortunately, there is no easy panacea for managers on how to motivate their staff. Organizations try to increase worker satisfaction with pay incentives and bonuses, giving individuals a say in decisions which affect them, and increasing the interest and responsibility of jobs. Different companies and different departments will all need to use different ways.

6.6 Summary

1 Motivating employees in an organization is difficult, but very important, as people who are motivated and satisfied with their jobs work harder and are more productive than those people who are dissatisfied with their jobs.
2 People are motivated by needs, wants, and fears.
3 Managers have to encourage a group of individuals with different personal priorities and goals to work together productively towards the company's goals.
4 Although there is an element of self-selection in matching personal goals and jobs, this is by no means always so.
5 Individuals will be motivated by different things at different stages in their careers and life, as personal priorities change.

6.7 Quick questions

1 What are the factors upon which a person's motivation is primarily dependent?
2 What is the difference between content motivation theories and process motivation theories?
3 Explain Maslow's hierarchy of needs.

4 How far does Herzberg's two-factor theory correspond to Maslow's need hierarchy?
5 According to expectancy theory, what does a person's level of motivation depend upon?
6 List some of the ways in which managers can motivate their staff.

7
Communicating

Communicating is a vital part of management. Without it, managers could not fulfil their other tasks. In this chapter the communication process, communication channels in organizations, and the impact of IT on communication systems and on management, are discussed.

7.1 Introduction

Communication can be defined as 'an attempt to achieve as complete and as accurate an understanding as possible between two or more people. It is an act characterised by a desire in one or more individuals to exchange information, ideas or feelings. This desire is implemented by using symbols, signs, actions, and pictures as well as other verbal and non-verbal elements in speaking and writing'. A more concise definition can be given as 'the process by which people attempt to share meaning *via* the transmission of symbolic messages'.

Communicating consists of an exchange of ideas and information. This exchange takes place between the organization and the surrounding environment (here communication can be seen as a means of connecting the organization with the outside world), and also inside the organization. Effective communications within a company are essential.

7.2 Management and communicating

Communicating is an integral part of the other elements of the management process. Indeed, it is only by communicating that managers can accomplish their other functions, of planning, organizing, controlling, and so on.

Communication and planning

We saw earlier that planning is instrumental in guiding the collective behaviour of an organization towards its intended objectives. The communication of information to the manager is essential to that planning process. Without accurate data and information managers cannot formulate relevant plans, and it is only through the communication process that plans are relayed down the organizational hierarchy to those subordinates and employees who have to implement the plans and meet the targets set out in them.

Communication and organizing

Similarly, managers need to communicate in order to organize. Organizing is aimed at prescribing specific activities which are required to achieve goals and objectives as identified within corporate plans. This organizing function again is heavily dependent on effective communications. They are needed to provide management with an understanding of the goals and objectives they are seeking to implement. Where organizing is the function of a team, then there must also be good communications within that team.

Communication and motivating

In order to motivate subordinates and staff, managers have to be able to communicate with them. Perhaps the aspect of communicating which is most important here is not the one only normally associated with bosses and their employees, i.e. downward communication from the manager to his subordinates, but, rather, upward communication. Communicating is always a two-way process, and although the image of managers is normally one of initiating communications, with others listening and receiving information, managers spend more time on the receiving end of communications. A good motivator and leader is one who listens to people.

Communication and control

Control and feedback were mentioned in Chapter 3 when planning was discussed. They comprise setting standards, monitoring performance and correcting deviations from the standards. Control and feedback obviously need the effective communication of information; they depend on its timing, its accuracy, and whether it is fed to the people who have the authority to take corrective action. Where the control process is in the hands of more than one person, then communication between them is also important.

Managing and communication

Communication is, therefore, a basic input and output for the functions of management. Communicating is also, in fact, synonymous with management, i.e. in managing one is communicating. Managers communicate with subordinates, peers, superiors, customers, suppliers, etc., by telephone, face-to-face meetings, electronic mail, and so on, as part of their daily work. One study by Rosemary Stewart of 160 managers over a 4-week period found that on average they spent two-thirds of their working time with other people – attending meetings, giving and receiving information and instructions, discussing matters with colleagues. Most of their remaining time tended to be spent preparing and reading reports. The study also found that middle-ranking and top managers could not work without interruption for more than half an hour once every 2 days (Stewart, *Managers and Their Jobs*, 1970).

The interrelation between communication and management can be summarized by modifying Alber's (1974) model of the management process (Figure 7.1).

The purpose of communicating

To sum up, there are a number of purposes of communicating which can be identified. These include:

1 *Decision-making*. Management is concerned with decision-making, and it can be said that the quality of those decisions is dependent to a large degree on the

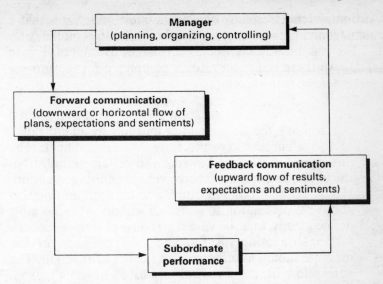

Figure 7.1   Interrelation between communication and management

quality of information communicated to the decision-makers.

2   *Organizing*. Another important purpose of communication is to start organizational processes in motion. These processes are concerned with acquiring resources, developing them, and transferring finished goods and services to the customers. All these processes depend on work teams and reporting relationships and, unless decisions are conveyed to and from the appropriate people, no tasks can be accomplished.

3   *Influencing*. The whole purpose of communicating is to persuade, inform, and educate. As such, its effect is to mould opinion.

4   *Activating*. Another purpose of communicating is to initiate action. Communication, in effect, acts as the regulating mechanism for beginning, continuing, and halting company business.

7.3 The communication process

To utilize the resources at its disposal properly, management must carefully develop and maintain an adequate communication system. Certainly one of the most basic skills that a management group must have is the ability to communicate.

The communication process consists of five stages (Figure 7.2). All these stages have to be completed for the process to be said to be a success:

1 *Perceive*. The communication process is centred around perception – the assignment of meaning by an individual to the stimuli he receives from his environment. The initiator of a message has received certain stimuli from the environment that he perceives as requiring attention. His purpose in communicating is to transmit information about his perception to a second person. Thus he must define clearly what he wishes to convey. If he is successful in structuring his thoughts, the recipient of the message should in turn perceive the need for action. The perception of the two individuals is never identical; rather, the communication is understood in similar ways by both parties through the use of commonly held symbols.

2 *Encode*. Once the individual originating the communication has clearly perceived and defined the thoughts he wants to convey, he has to put these thoughts into a code, using communication symbols that will be understood by the recipient. It is important that the originator of the communication expresses his thoughts, intentions, and impressions by means of symbols which accurately represent the message he wishes to give to the recipient. These symbols can be written, verbal or take other forms, e.g. expression, demeanour, etc.

3 *Transmit*. Transmission is the conveyance of communication symbols from the message's originator to its receiver, either verbally or non-verbally. The selection of the means of transmission must be made after due consideration of cost, speed, accuracy, physical distance between the two parties, the need for 'personal' messages, and the type and quality of transmission media available.

4 *Receive and decode*. Once the originator has sent out his message, the receiver must assign meaning to it. Thus the receiver must decode the message. This is essential, since the meaning that the receiver assigns to the mess-

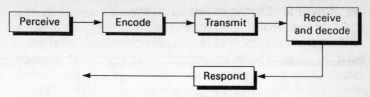

Figure 7.2   The communication process

age governs the extent to which the communication has been successful. If the receiver either does not or cannot understand what the originator of the message is trying to convey, then communication has not been a success.

5   *Response*. The final step in the communication process is one of recycling. The receiver of the message considers the response he will make to the communication. This response will show just how well the original perception and message have been conveyed.

Data and information

It must be noted that, with regard to the human communication process, differentiation needs to be made between data and information. As far as human communication is concerned, information can be defined as data which have meaning to the receiver. Data which do not convey meaning to the receiver are the equivalent of nonsense.

One purpose of communicating which has already been mentioned is to affect the behaviour of the receiving person. Therefore it is a mistake for managers to assume that communication has been accomplished once the data have been transmitted. Transmission does not guarantee that the meaning intended by the originator has been conveyed. Both the receiver of the message and the person transmitting it can affect the meaning ultimately communicated. The transmitting person has only limited control over what the receiving person will perceive, while the receiver, by reason of personal psychological nature and background, or because of 'noise' in the communication process, may see no meaning at all in the message, or may even assign to it an incorrect meaning.

7.4 Rules for effective communications

Although there are many possible standards that can be used to judge the effectiveness of a system of communication, speed, accuracy, and cost serve as representative measures. Businesses today demand rapid communications and accurate information systems. Decisions often have to be made at short notice, because of the dynamic nature of environmental conditions. Nevertheless, these decisions must be based on adequate information. Therefore the communication system used by the organization must be capable of conveying large quantities of information quickly to and from the data sources and the decision-makers. At the same time, the system must be capable of transmitting accurate and timely information to the places that need it.

Criteria for good communications

Effective communications are not solely a function of an effective communication system. We need to look also at the criteria for, or principles of, good communications, irrespective of the system by which they are transmitted. The American Management Association (AMA) has suggested the following as principles of good communications:

1   The communicator must clarify his/her ideas before communicating.
2   The true purpose of each message or communication must be examined.
3   Consideration must be given to the total physical and human setting in which the communication is made.
4   There needs to be consultation with others in planning communications, so conflicting or unintelligible messages are not sent.
5   The communicator needs to be mindful of the overtones of the message which he/she is communicating, as well as its basic content.
6   Opportunities should be taken to convey something of help or value to the receiver.
7   Communications should be followed up to check that the intended meaning has been understood.
8   Communications should not be determined solely by

the needs of the present, but the communicator should also have tomorrow in mind.

9 Actions need to support communications, or else conflicting and contradictory messages will be transmitted to the receiver.

10 Good communications depend on a willingness to listen and understand.

Principles for good communications

In addition we can also identify the following principles required for effective communications:

1 *Integrity*. The integrity of an enterprise depends in part on supporting the position of subordinate managers. Since they occupy centres of communication networks, they should be encouraged to use their positions for this purpose. Thus it is important that superiors do not go over the heads of their subordinates by contacting employees directly, unless unavoidable.

2 *Clarity*. The sender of a message has the responsibility to formulate the communication and express it in an understandable way. This should help overcome barriers to communication, such as badly expressed memos, faulty translations and transmissions, unclarified assumptions, etc.

3 *Trust*. The key to effective interpersonal communications is trust. Employees will not send accurate and open messages to their supervisor unless they trust that supervisor. They must have confidence that the supervisor will not use the information they have sent to the employees' detriment. They must believe that the information will not be inappropriately or inaccurately transferred to others.

7.5 Barriers to effective communications

We have seen the importance of communication for unifying activity and effecting change in an organization. In light of this it is important to understand how barriers to good communications can spring up, and the problems that they cause, making communicating less effective than it needs to be. These barriers may be identified and explained as follows.

Lack of preparation

A failure to prepare adequately reduces the effectiveness of communications. This failure usually arises from a belief that there exists a ready-made package of information which needs only to be directed towards the appropriate recipients to effect the required change. This is a mistaken belief. Time and thought need to be given to communicating. The person initiating the message needs to be clear about his/her objective, needs to consider alternatives, and then select the form of the message. A conscious choice of communication techniques must then be made. Receivers must also be prepared to listen or to accept the information given them.

Lack of clarity

Another problem with communicating lies in the tendency for vagueness and lack of clarity. A frequent consequence of this is costly errors and costly correction processes.

Assumptions

Unclarified assumptions which underlie many messages also cause problems and prevent effective communications.

Premature evaluation

Rogers and Roethlisberger in *Barriers and Gateways to Communication* point to the tendency to jump to conclusions prematurely when receiving information, instead of keeping an uncompromised position and then judging the message objectively.

Differing cultures and backgrounds

The problems caused by different social backgrounds, different cultures (both organizational cultures and social cultures), age differences and so on, which prevent clear communications between parties, should never be underestimated.

7.6 Communication channels

There are two basic kinds of communication channels which exist in organizations: formal channels and informal channels.

Formal channels

Formal channels are those that are officially designated and recognized by the organization for the transmission of official messages within or outside it. The formal channels of communication are determined by the organization's structure and the organizational chart. This describes the official lines of authority, power, responsibility, and accountability in the organization. All these relationships rely on communication. For instance, the exercising of authority can be viewed as a downward flow of information from a manager to a subordinate. Communication through formal channels can be complicated, however, by the fact that a subordinate does not communicate in the same way with his manager as with his peers.

Informal channels

An informal communication network is essential for the successful operation of a company. A typical informal network comprises members within the same level of the organization, and (depending on how formal or informal the general organizational structure and atmosphere are) can include employees at different levels of seniority. It cannot replace a formal network, but it can complement and enhance it.

Formal v informal

The formal network is often static, while the organization it seeks to activate is dynamic, and must react quickly to changing situations. The informal network, commonly known as 'the grapevine', is flexible and able to carry information with amazing speed and accuracy. Thus it acts as a very beneficial, rapid problem-solver in many companies.

Team briefing

The formal and informal communication channels tend to meet in team briefing groups. These groups are small (usually less than thirty people) and are arranged on a regulated but informal basis. The communicator is of higher status than the rest of the group – a foreman or manager – and the purpose of the meetings is to inform the group of what is happening within the organization, what is expected of them, and so on. This downward communication is important, but so is the informal feedback which results from this face-to-face contact and discussion. Team briefings and discussion also help to improve employees' morale and commitment, as they are able to feel that they can make more of a personal contribution to the organization.

7.7 Information technology and communications

The IT revolution has had a significant impact on communications within organizations and on their managers. At a minimum, the latest communications and computer technology enable businesses to deliver information and data far more quickly to the people who need it, and at a lower cost, than they ever could before. The latest technology in digital computers can transmit everything – voice, data, or image – by converting them into a stream of computer on-off pulses, and communication networks are now being updated to become multi-functional links carrying everything from 'phone calls to television pictures. At the same time new ways of sending digital information are dramatically lowering the cost of sending messages vast distances.

The spread of powerful personal computers throughout businesses and organizations, together with an array of sophisticated software packages, mean that managers at virtually all department levels have access to accurate, highly detailed information and figures, e.g. on sales levels of product X, broken down into regions. This *should* lead to better planning and decision-making, and tighter control over variances from those plans. However, often managers become swamped with too much information, simply because of the availability of the detailed figures, and poor communication systems which do not provide managers with the information reports appropriate to their needs, position, and seniority. The detail in reports, like the plans the reports give feedback on, should be inversely proportional to the seniority of the manager. Details of weekly sales and calls made by each sales representative in an area should be provided to the area sales manager, not to the company's sales and marketing director.

7.8 Summary

1 Good management depends upon good communications, both by communication systems (providing information through formal channels up and down the company) and personal communication between peers, subordinates and superiors.
2 Barriers preventing good communications include lack of clarity in plans, etc.; badly prepared and thought out communications; the different backgrounds of people, leading to misunderstandings; and the assumption that once a message has been given, it has been understood and the communication process has been successful.
3 Organizations need both formal communication processes and channels and informal ones to provide feedback and comment.

7.9 Quick questions

1 Why is a good communications system so vital for good management?
2 Identify the main purposes of communication.
3 Identify and describe the elements in the communication process.
4 How may effective communications be hindered?
5 What are an organization's formal communication channels determined by?

8
Control

The chapter covers how control links in with other management functions, control processes and techniques, control systems and MIS, and quality control.

8.1 The concept of control

The managerial function of control is the measurement and correction of the performance of subordinates' activities and production processes, to make sure that the enterprise's objectives and plans are being accomplished.

8.2 The process of control

The basic control process consists of three steps: establishing standards, measuring performance against these standards, and correcting any deviations from these targets which occur.

Establishing standards

Planning is a prerequisite for effective control; without planning there can be no pre-determined understanding of the results desired by the organization. The first logical step in the control process is therefore to draw up objectives and plans. Yet as company plans vary in both detail and complexity, and since managers cannot usually monitor everything, special standards are established.

What are standards?

Standards are, by definition, simply criteria of performance. They are the selected points in an entire planning pro- gramme where measurements of performance are made, so as to give managers signals as to how things are going without having to watch and monitor every step in the process.

Standards are variable. Among the best are verifiable goals or objectives, whether stated in quantitative or quali- tative terms, regularly set in well-operated management by objective systems. As the end results which subordinates are responsible for are the best measures of the achievement of the plans, they furnish excellent standards of control. These goal standards can also be stated in physical terms, such as quantities of goods produced, and so can be easily checked.

Measurement of performance

The measurement of performance achieved against the standards set should (ideally) be on a forward looking basis, so that deviations from the standards may be detected in advance of their happening, and avoided by appropriate remedial action.

When measurement is difficult

If standards are appropriately drawn up, and if the means are available for determining exactly what subordinates are doing, appraisal of actual or expected performance is fairly easy. There are, however, many activities for which it is difficult to develop accurate standards, and many which are hard to measure. If an item is mass-produced then it may be simple to establish labour–hour standards and to measure performance against them. But if the item is custom-made, the appraisal of performance is often a far more difficult task. Moreover, in the less technical kinds of work, not only may standards be hard to develop, but appraisal may also be difficult. For example, measuring the performance of the finance vice-president or the industrial relations director is not easy, because definite standards are very difficult to set.

Nevertheless, as managers at all levels develop verifiable objectives, stated in either quantitative or qualitative terms, these become the standards against which all position performance in the organization's hierarchy can be measured.

The importance of information

An accurate measurement of performance depends heavily on the relevance, accuracy and timeliness of information or feedback. The supply of such information comes from a variety of sources within the organization. The single most important source is the management accounting department, which is responsible for producing regular operating statements, expenditure analyses, profit forecasts, cashflow statements, and other relevant information used for control.

Correcting deviations

The manager's task of correcting deviations is made easier if standards which reflect the organizational structure are set, and if performance is measured in these terms, since he will then know exactly where, in the assignment of individual or group duties, the corrective measures must be applied.

Control as part of management

The correction of deviations in performance is the point at which control can be seen as part of the whole system of management, and where it relates to the other functions of management. Managers can correct deviations by redrawing their plans or by modifying their goals, or by exercising their organizing function, through a reassignment or clarification of duties. They may also seek to correct deviations by recruiting additional staff, by better selection and training of subordinates, or by firing employees.

Programmes of correction

Once the deviations have been identified and analysed, the manager must develop a programme for corrective action and implement it, in order to arrive at the desired performance. The development and the implementation of corrective programmes are likely to be time-consuming tasks. For example, in the case of quality control, it may take a considerable time to discover exactly what the cause of factory rejects is, and more time to put corrective measures into effect. This time lag in the management control process shows how important future directed control is, if control is to be effective. What managers need for effective management control is a control system that tells them, in time to take corrective action, that problems will occur if they do not do something about them now.

The control process is illustrated in Figure 8.1.

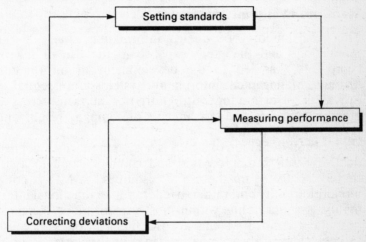

Figure 8.1 The control process

8.3 Control information

Effective control is dependent on the generation and supply of relevant information. The qualities of good control information are as follows:

1 *Accuracy*. Accurate control information is necessary to direct the attention of the manager to the matters actually requiring control action. If the information is inaccurate, then the manager is liable to make incorrect and inappropriate control decisions.
2 *Timeliness*. The characteristic of timeliness is important,

since it is of little consolation to the manager to know that, although the information was accurate, it arrived too late to be of use. Timely information will avoid control delays and encourage prompt control action.

3   *Conciseness*. Management information systems can produce vast quantities of information, but the manager needs relevant information which highlights the exceptional items requiring attention.

4   *Comprehensiveness*. The information presented needs to provide a complete picture of events to prevent an inappropriate control decision.

Management information systems

The provision of good quality information, thanks to IT innovations and the great expanse in the use of micro-computers, has led to the development of information systems. Management information systems are essential to provide information for control purposes, allowing access to greater databases and fast analysis of company results and possible future trends.

One brief definition of a MIS is 'a system in which defined data are collected, processed and communicated to assist those responsible for the use of resources'. A MIS is not a monolithic entity but, rather, a federation of functional information systems. Thus within most organizations the most prominent control systems are the financial ones, because success is almost always measured in monetary terms.

Control reports

The purpose of control systems and their information is to produce control reports. The information contained within these should, firstly, have a purpose (and be relevant to that purpose) and, secondly, be tailored to meet the needs of the appropriate manager. There should be a hierarchy of control reports, so that each manager in the organization is made responsible for the activities over which he has authority.

Control and feedback

The information generated by control systems is known as feedback. This feedback is usually produced on results.

Actual performance is recorded and information fed back to the managers responsible for achieving the target performance. Early feedback is essential for accurate control, especially where unexpected deviations have occurred.

To be effective the feedback reporting system must be designed to provide quick, accurate reports of any serious deviations from the planned performance levels. The system must also supply reports to the correct level within the organization and be phrased in the same terms as the plan. In addition, the feedback must reflect the needs of the company. We can categorize feedback into two types:

1 *Positive feedback*. This causes the system to repeat or to further intensify the particular condition being considered.
2 *Negative feedback*. This causes the system to report and correct a trend by taking action in the opposite direction. A control system which uses negative feedback is often referred to as 'homeostatic' in character.

8.4 Requirements for adequate controls

To sum up this section, if controls are to be effective, they must meet certain requirements. These are:

1 The controls should be tailored to positions. For example, what will do for a vice-president in charge of manufacturing will certainly not be appropriate for a shop foreman.
2 Controls should reflect the structure of the organization. The more controls are designed to reflect the place in the organization where responsibility for action lies, the more they will facilitate corrective action being taken as and when it is needed.
3 Controls should be tailored to the personalities of individual managers.
4 Controls should be objective.
5 Controls should be flexible.
6 Controls should be economical. Control techniques and approaches are efficient when they detect and illuminate

the causes of actual or potential deviations from plans, with the minimum of costs incurred in developing them.

8.5 Control techniques

Although the fundamental nature and purpose of management control does not change, a variety of tools and techniques have been used over the years to help managers control the organization. Some are quite basic, while others are more complex and sophisticated. Some measure the firm's financial soundness, while others are concerned with production efficiency. Still other control tools deal with employee attitudes and perceptions. Although control devices vary widely in their design and in what they measure, they all seek the same basic objective: to determine variations from desired standards so that managers can take appropriate corrective action.

Budgetary control

A budget is a statement, usually expressed in financial terms, of the desired performance of an organization in the pursuit of its objectives in the short term. It is an action plan for the company's immediate future, representing the operational and tactical sections of the corporate plan. Budgetary control takes the targets of desired performance as its standards, then systematically collates information relating to actual performance and so identifies any variances between the target performance and the actual performance.

Standard costs and variance analysis

Standard costing is the calculation of how much costs, such as those for materials, labour, production, etc., should be under set conditions. It is these costs which form the basis for the costs in budgets. Variance analysis is the examination and investigation of the factors which have caused any difference between the standard costs set and the results actually achieved, in an attempt to eliminate waste and inefficiency.

Budgetary control systems

A budgetary control system is built up with the following basic steps:

1 *Forecasts* – statements of probable sales, costs and other relevant financial and quantitative data.
2 *Sales budget*. The preparation of a sales budget is based on an analysis of past sales and a forecast of future sales in the light of a number of assumptions about market trends.
3 *A production budget*. This is prepared on the basis of the sales budget. It is an assessment of the productive capacity of the enterprise in the light of the estimates of sales, and a consequential adjustment of either (or both) to ensure a reasonable balance between demand and potential supply. Production budgets will include output targets, and cost estimates relating to labour and materials.
4 *Capital expenditure budget*. The capital expenditure budget specifically outlines proposed capital expenditure on plant, machinery, equipment, etc. Capital expenditure budgets should usually be tied in with long-range planning, because capital resources and investment in plant and equipment usually require a long period for their costs to be recovered from operations, which creates a high degree of inflexibility.
5 *Cash budget*. This is simply a forecast of cash receipts and disbursements, against which actual cash receipts, etc., are measured. This is perhaps the single most important control of a company, as the availability of cash to meet obligations as they fall due is the first requirement of existence. See Table 8.1.

It can be said that if budgetary controls are to work well, managers need to remember that they are designed only as tools, and not to replace managing. Moreover, they are tools of all managers, not just those of the budget controller. It must also be noted that to be most effective, budget-making and administration must receive the wholehearted support of top management.

Table 8.1 A cash budget

	Jan. (£)	Feb. (£)	March (£)	April (£)	May (£)	June (£)
Receipts:						
Sales	10,000	10,000	13,000	21,000	32,000	40,000
Total receipts	10,000	10,000	13,000	21,000	32,000	40,000
Payments for goods	5,000	7,000	9,000	9,000	12,000	17,000
Wages	2,000	2,000	3,000	4,000	5,000	5,000
Income tax			3,000			5,000
Dividends	1,000			1,000		
Capital outlay	3,000				3,000	
Total expenditure	11,000	9,000	15,000	14,000	20,000	27,000
Net cash inflow/outflow	(1,000)	1,000	(2,000)	7,000	12,000	13,000

Break-even analysis

Break-even analysis is a valuable and relatively simple technique for managerial planning and control. A break-even chart (Figure 8.2) shows how different levels of sales affect the profits of a company. The chart produces a break-even point, which is the level of operations where income and costs are equal. Sales levels above the break-even point are profitable; whereas sales levels below the break-even point are not.

Certain assumptions have to be made in the use of these charts. Among these is the acceptance of a static environment, when in fact the environment is more likely a dynamic one. There is also an implied assumption that the revenue/cost relationship is linear. Nor can the chart be used beyond the budget period of the firm. Despite these limitations, break-even charts do have a basic practical value – if only as a first approximation of the profitability of a project.

Network analysis

The aim of network analysis is to ensure that the shortest possible time elapses between a project's inception and completion, to keep delay and cost to an absolute minimum. Thus a diagrammatic network of 'events' is drawn up in sequential order, with a time-scale for each part. The total

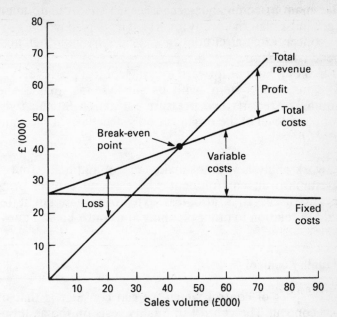

Figure 8.2 Break-even chart

time is determined by the shortest way home, by taking the critical path.

The network can be highly complicated, the critical path threading its way through a veritable maze of highways and byways to achieve a minimum sequence of significant events. Such a highly complex network usually requires the use of a computer to deal with assessment, analysis, and scheduling of input data. Whatever the type of network, the programme or project must be effectively controlled throughout the sequence of scheduled activities to ensure satisfactory progress as planned.

The advantages of network analysis

Network analysis carries with it five important advantages:

1 It forces managers to plan, because it is impossible to make a time–event analysis without planning and seeing how the pieces fit together.
2 It forces planning throughout the company and down

the chain of command, because each subordinate manager must plan the event for which he is responsible.
3 It concentrates attention on critical elements that may need correction.
4 It makes a kind of forward looking control possible.
5 The network system, with its sub-systems, makes the aiming of reports and pressure for action, at the right spot and level in the organization's structure, at the right time, possible.

Network analysis will not make control automatic, but it does establish an environment where sound control principles are used. It is also less expensive than might be thought in relation to other planning and control techniques.

8.6 Quality control

A final aspect of control which we can consider is that of quality control. The control of quality rests on the assumption that in mass-production no two units are exactly identical, but that it is possible to mass-produce vast quantities of almost identical units. These units can be produced within certain tolerances, and a customer will accept variations between these tolerances, but not outside them. The role of quality control is to ensure that appropriate standards of quality are set and that variances beyond the tolerances are rejected. Quality control therefore is basically a system for setting quality standards, measuring performance against those standards and taking appropriate action to deal with deviations outside the permitted tolerances.

Quality control activities traditionally can be very costly. Since they represent an overhead in the production area, the degree of time and resources spent on them tend to be related to factors such as price, consistency, safety and legal requirements.

One answer is for companies to initiate programmes of 'total quality control', such as those that have been part of many Japanese manufacturing companies for some time. Japanese firms, notably in the car industry, instill a concern for extremely high quality throughout their production processes, and in all their employees. Each person on the shop floor is personally responsible for checking and testing the quality of the goods that he or she makes. The aim, ultimately, is to achieve zero defects in goods manufactured in the production process, making everything right first time around. This means that the cost of rejecting goods and reworking parts which do not meet the given tolerance levels should be eliminated.

Of course setting up and initiating a total quality control programme is costly and time-consuming: the workforce has to be trained to check and inspect the parts and goods they make, and generally has to be trained to high standards of workmanship. The management also has to seek out and put right underlying causes of damage and rework, instead of accepting wastage, provided it is kept below certain level, as unavoidable and inevitable. However, firms that have initiated such programmes have shown that in the longer term they allow the firm to be extremely cost-effective, competitive, and able to use the quality of their goods to a very effective marketing advantage.

8.7 Summary

1 Control comprises setting standards, measuring how far actual results meet those standards, and using this feedback to correct any deviations between the two.
2 Feedback used has to be accurate, timely, concise, and comprehensive.
3 As most standards tend to be set in monetary terms (being a common, understandable and measurable unit throughout the organization), budgets tend to be much used in control systems.

8.8 Quick questions

1 Identify and describe the stages in the control process.
2 What are the qualities needed in information reports in order to produce good control procedures?
3 Explain how a budgetary control system may be constructed.
4 What are the advantages of using network analysis?
5 Define 'total quality control'.

9
Decision-making

It can be said that making decisions is the whole point of management. This chapter will look at the decision-making process, and how it fits in with the rest of the manager's functions. Various techniques of decision-making, and the importance of information and the use of IT and computers will also be looked at.

9.1 Introduction

Decision-making is the process of thought and action that leads to a decision. It lies at the heart of managing any enterprise or business, and (like communicating) it has a bearing on all the other functions of management. Managers spend their time choosing between alternative courses of action on the basis of the information they have available at the time, i.e. making decisions.

The classical concept of rational, economic decision-making assumes that the decision-maker:

1 Has complete knowledge of all the possible alternative courses of action.
2 Has complete knowledge of the consequences of taking every alternative.
3 Can attach definite payoffs or utilities to each possible outcome.
4 Can order the payoffs of each course of action in a unique sequence from highest to lowest payoff.

The above assumptions are rarely completely valid, because of the following factors:

(a) Uncertainty – there are two aspects to this problem. First, possible alternative courses of action may not be known or identifiable, and, second, the outcomes and payoffs of any individual course of action may be uncertain.

(b) The decision-maker may have many criteria, both quantifiable and unquantifiable, by which he wishes to value a possible course of action.

(c) There may be practical limitations on the analysis of alternatives. The decision-maker may lack the mental capacity to evaluate and compare all the possible alternatives. In addition, a search and evaluation of all possible alternatives is usually impracticable on the grounds of the limited time and resources that can be brought to bear on any one decision.

9.2 Criteria for good decision-making

Perhaps the most serious difficulty in decision-making is the existence of unquantifiable objectives. Janis and Mann (1977) have recognized this problem and have suggested making the assumption that a decision is likely to be more satisfactory when the quality of the decision-making procedure is high. Seven major criteria can be used to determine whether decision-making procedures are of a high quality:

1 The identification of a wide range of alternative courses of action.

2 Surveying the full range of objectives to be used and the values implied by the choice being made.

3 A careful consideration of the costs and risks of both positive and negative consequences that could follow from each alternative.

4 An intense search for new information relevant to the further evaluation of the alternatives.

5 The assimilation of any new information, even when that information or judgement does not support the course of action initially preferred.

6 The re-examination of the positive and negative conse-

quences of all known alternatives before making a final choice.
7   Making detailed provisions for implementing the chosen course of action, including contingency plans in the event that various known risks were actually to occur.

Janis and Mann use the term 'vigilant information processing' (VIP) to describe a decision process where all seven criteria have been met to the best of the decision maker's ability.

9.3 Stages in the decision-making process

Decision-making proceeds in several stages. These are:

1   Diagnose and define the problem. This calls for distinguishing between conditions which are 'musts' and conditions which are 'shoulds'. A staffing problem can be analysed as 'We *must* employ someone who can do the job at the given salary, and they *should* fit in well with others in the organization'.
2   Gather and analyse the relevant facts. This includes finding out who will have the most experience of the problem and information about it.
3   Develop alternatives. This is a natural extension to the previous stage of fact-gathering, and many possible solutions will arise naturally from it. However, it remains a danger that the first feasible solution will be accepted rather than a choice made between a number of them.
4   Evaluate the alternative solutions in terms of the organizational objectives.
5   Select the best alternative. The choice will be based on the available information and will usually be a compromise between the various factors considered. Drucker (1955) suggests four factors which should be used to judge possible solutions against each other:

(*a*)   The risk compared to the expected gain.
(*b*)   The amount of effort each alternative solution requires.

(*c*) The timing of each alternative, especially whether a one-step-at-a-time approach is fine, or if dramatic changes are needed immediately.

(*d*) The availability of any additional resources needed.

6 Analyse the possible consequences of the decision to enable any anticipated problems to be successfully dealt with. For example, there may be resistance to change within the organization or there may be a need for additional funding.

7 Implement the decision. This will include setting up a budget and defining responsibilities to ensure the completion of the task. There needs to be a system of checking and control to ensure the decision is accepted and implemented by subordinates and other members of the organization.

Problem-solving and decision-making

Decision-making encompasses the management function of planning and is similar in some respects to problem-solving. Luthans (1981) describes problem-solving as 'any goal-directed activity that must overcome some type of barrier to accomplish the goal'. Problem-solving is thus a more extensive activity than decision-making, and it is the need to solve problems that frequently gives rise to the need for decisions. Unfortunately, in problem-solving, the emphasis is too often placed exclusively on obtaining answers, when it is also important to be sure that the right problem has been identified.

Steps in the problem-solving process

Elbing (1980) describes managerial problem-solving as a five-step process:

1 The manager perceives a problem, perhaps without a clear rational reason for doing so.

2 The manager responds by attempting to diagnose the causes of the problem.

3   In addition the manager must attempt to define the nature of the problem.
4   The selection of a method of solution (including a decision-making process).
5   Implementation of the chosen course of action, whether or not it actually leads to a solution of the problem.

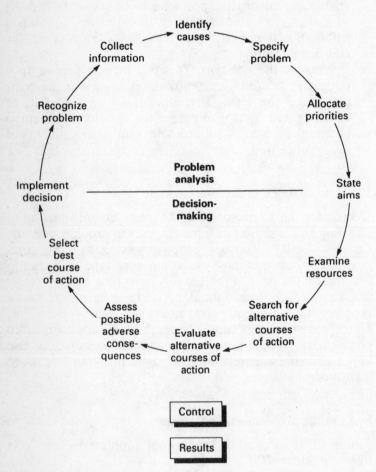

Figure 9.1   Steps in problem analysis and decision-making

Steps in decision-making

Figure 9.1 illustrates the following steps.

Statement of aims

A clear understanding of the objectives to be achieved or the *real* problem to be solved is necessary, particularly where a number of managers participate in the decision process.

Examination of resources

Any examination should cover three basic, critical resources:

1 *Human resources*. Who is available to help? Who is, and who is not, trained? How many persons are available to carry out extra work?
2 *Financial resources*. What can be spent? What are the limits of financial authority? What is the extent of unused budget funds available for this problem?
3 *Physical resources*. Where can the work be done? Are materials and equipment available?

Searching for alternatives

Four guidelines are suggested in connection with the search for alternative courses of action:

(*a*) Use knowledge and experience already available. Ready-made solutions often already exist, tabulated and written up in reports.
(*b*) Ask penetrating questions.
(*c*) Apply problem analysis techniques.
(*d*) Think creatively.

Evaluation of alternatives

Evaluating the alternatives, to begin with, calls for an assessment of how well the desirable needs are met. The next part is concerned with assessing the advantages and disadvantages of each possible alternative to arrive at a balanced decision.

9.4 Techniques used for decision analysis

The techniques used to evaluate possible solutions to find the most suitable include the following methods.

Marginal or incremental costing

This technique compares the additional revenues generated by each possible scheme with how much each will cost. It is useful, because variables are emphasized rather than constants and averages. However, it is sometimes very difficult to quantify adequately the benefits which may result (especially if the project under consideration is a long-term, radical one), and all the costs which could be incurred.

Discounted cashflow appraisal

DCF methods are probably the most widely used appraisal techniques. They are based on the premise that money received now is worth more than money received at some point in the future, because of such factors as inflation and because cash received now can earn interest in the intervening period.

The two main methods of DCF analysis are finding a project's net present value and calculating its internal rate of return. Calculating the NPV is accomplished by discounting all the project's forecasted future net cashflows to their present value. The IRR of the project is the discount rate which gives an NPV of zero. In investment terms, if the IRR of a project is greater than the firm's cost of capital, then it is worth undertaking. When evaluating possible alternatives, you will find that both methods enable projects' profitability over the course of their lifetimes to be compared.

Cost–benefit analysis

This evaluation technique is used when data cannot be quantified, but when such things as the social benefits and costs of a possible project (such as pollution or unemployment) are important in making the decision. The method weighs the effectiveness of each alternative in meeting the scheme's objectives against its potential costs.

Sensitivity analysis

With sensitivity analysis the assumptions behind each plan are questioned to see how valid they are. The dependence of the plan on each assumption is also assessed, to find out what degree of risk is being taken and on how sound a basis. The technique has the advantage of being easy to use, especially with spreadsheet computer packages.

Risk analysis

Risk analysis gauges what the range of each variable is and the probability of it occurring, e.g. the chances of the cost price exceeding or falling below the best estimate and by how much.

Decision trees

Decision trees (such as the Vroom–Yetton leadership model) are conceptual maps of sequences of possible decisions and their outcomes. With the probability of each outcome occurring added too, the riskiness of each course of action, and the possible payoffs from each can be assessed.

Linear programming

This is a mathematically based technique of determining the best combination of limited resources which can achieve the set objectives. It is especially useful where objectives can be measured and data quantified, e.g. in allocating jobs to machines when different jobs take different times and the machines have number limits.

The advantages of decision-making techniques

All the techniques detailed above try to attribute values or costs (in one way or another) to different courses of action. Some often take account of risk or the probability of loss. The use of decision analysis has the following advantages:

1 It focuses thinking on the critical elements of the decision.
2 It helps to structure problems and facilitates organized thought.
3 It uncovers hidden assumptions behind a decision and clarifies its logical implications.
4 It simplifies the consideration of alternatives.
5 It provides an effective vehicle for communication.
6 It identifies areas where additional information is needed.
7 It provides a framework for contingency planning.

Selecting the best course of action

Although we can trace a sequence of logical thought processes, at the time of decision the logic may not be explicit. The decision-maker will in effect be putting a value on those factors which cannot be formally evaluated, and which may therefore have been omitted from the earlier stages we have been considering. The mark of a good manager is 'flair' – that innate sense, possibly developed through long experience, of the illogicalities in people's behaviour and of the element of chance in the business environment.

Implementation

A decision is of no value to the business, indeed it might be said for practical purposes not to exist, until it has been put into effect. The moment at which the decision has to be converted into a plan of action provides the true test of confidence in the decision process, because it is then that money, people and other resources are going to be committed. A systematic approach to the whole process of problem analysis and decision-making is essential if only for this purpose – to give managers the confidence to initiate action.

9.5 The behavioural theory of decision-making

The behavioural theory of decision-making was first advanced by Cyert and March. The satisficing nature of many decision-makers was then also recognized and put forward by Simon (1957), who proposed a more realistic 'administrative man' alternative to the classic rational, economic decision-maker. The decision-making behaviour of Simon's 'administrative man' can be summarized as follows:

1 In choosing between alternatives, decision-makers look for a scheme which provides a satisfactory payoff rather than the best possible payoff.
2 The decision-maker recognizes that his perception of the world is only a dramatically simplified model of the real world.
3 A satisficer can make a choice without first determining all the possible alternatives and without ascertaining that these are actually all the alternatives.

Satisficing decisions

Furthermore, Simon proposed that decision-makers (satisficers) simplify the decision process in various ways, in order to define the decision within the bounds of their mental capacities. Thus a decision-maker limits his search to the identification of a course of action that merely satisfies some minimum set of requirements. The examination of a large number of alternatives is not precluded, but alternatives are examined sequentially, and the first satisfactory one evaluated is usually the alternative selected.

9.6 Decision-making and planning

Ackoff (1970) notes that planning is a special kind of decision-making process, with three particular characteristics:

1 Planning is anticipatory decision-making. 'It is a process of deciding what to do and how to do it before action is required.' Planning is necessary because it takes time to decide what to do and how to achieve certain desired aims.
2 Planning produces a set of interdependent decisions. Such a set of decisions may be too large to handle all at once and must therefore be dealt with in stages. Decisions made in the earlier stages affect later

decisions, yet these early decisions may have to be reviewed in the light of decisions taken in later stages.
3 Planning is directed towards outcomes which would not otherwise occur. In particular, it is concerned with avoiding inappropriate action and reducing the failure to exploit opportunities.

Like planning, different levels of management have to make different types of decision, with different amounts of uncertainty and with varying time spans. Supervisors and junior levels of management have (usually) fairly clear decisions to make, where the problems and their solutions are routine. The decisions made at this level usually have to be made quickly, with their success (or otherwise) known quickly too.

As managers progress up the company hierarchy, the decisions they have to make have longer time spans between the problem being noted and the results of their decisions becoming known. Decisions are also subject to more and more uncertainty and risk, and the consequences of a wrong decision is more and more costly. Delegation to subordinates is often used to try to prepare less senior managers for taking such decisions.

9.7 Information and information technology

Any decisions made can only be as good as the information on which they are based. If managers receive wrong, unclear data on a problem, or if they do not receive all the information that they need, then the solution they decide upon is liable to be a poor one. Overloading managers with data on a problem is almost as bad as not providing them with sufficient information to base a decision on. Too much data will mean that significant information is often overlooked – lost among the superfluous facts and figures. To avoid this, the organization has to develop a good information processing system which provides its managers with relevant, timely and accurate information, both from the outside environment, and from inside the company in the form of feedback and control reports.

Management information systems do not have to be IT-based, but micro-computer systems do allow managers to access into all the information that they need instantly, and can allow them to work out the consequences of alternative solutions before the decision is taken. They may thereby avoid costly and irreversible errors of judgement.

Routine decisions to routine problems can be programmed into a computer system. This will allow corrective measures to be taken quickly and easily, e.g. the automatic re-ordering of materials when items in stock fall to a certain level, thus helping prevent expensive stock-outs, and freeing employees for more important, non-routine tasks.

9.8 Summary

1 The whole task of management is focused on taking decisions, about the running of the business and its future goals, and about the company's employees – how to organize them, how to lead and motivate them, how to train and develop their full abilities, etc.

2 Most decisions, especially those taken by lower levels of management, are fairly routine ones, and are encountered many, many times.

3 The decisions taken by senior managers are of a different nature, and call for choosing between different, often risky strategies, in order to solve ill-defined and unclear problems.

4 There are a variety of decision analysis techniques and tools, and decision-making processes, to help managers make these second types of decision, or at least to reduce the risk of making costly mistakes.

5 Good decisions are based on good information: an effective and efficient MIS should improve the quality of decisions at all levels of the organization.

9.9 Quick questions

1 Identify the assumptions behind the theory of rational economic decision-making.

2 Why are these assumptions invalid?

3 Describe the stages in the decision-making process.
4 Detail some of the techniques commonly used in decision-making.
5 Why are decision analysis techniques used?
6 In what way is planning a type of decision-making?

10
Personnel management

This chapter will cover the areas of personnel recruitment, selection, training programmes, and another important aspect of personnel management – employment legislation. Management performance appraisal will be discussed in Chapter 12.

10.1 The role of personnel management

Personnel management, according to the Institute of Personnel Management, is the process of management concerned with

> recruiting and selecting people; training and developing them for their work; ensuring that their payment and conditions of employment are appropriate, where necessary negotiating such terms of employment with trade unions; advising on healthy and appropriate working conditions; the organization of people at work, and the encouragement of relations between management and work people.

Although many medium and larger-sized companies will have specialist personnel managers in separate departments, the Institute's definition of personnel management above, shows that it should be regarded as another function of general management, like planning and controlling.

The key areas of personnel management are the recruitment and selection of new employees, their training and development, and ensuring that the company complies with all employment legislation. Other areas, such as job enrichment, job enlargement, and motivating employees, have been covered earlier.

10.2 Recruitment

A distinction should be made between the recruitment of potential employees and their selection. The aim of recruitment is to ensure that the organization's demand for manpower is met by attracting potential employees in a cost-effective and timely manner. The selection process is then used to identify, from these potential employees, those individuals who seem most likely to fulfil the requirements of the organization (both in the short and long term preferably).

Recruitment procedures

The recruitment procedures of an organization often embody a particular code of conduct. Thus, for example, an organization will, wherever possible, advertise posts internally before it advertises externally. When it does advertise externally, it will advertise under the company name, providing details of the vacancy and conditions of employment. It may also seek to inform the candidates of their progress in the recruitment procedure.

When a company is seeking to fill a post, the first step should be to define and describe the precise nature and duties of the job. This can be very difficult, as the existing formal job description may well not cover all the extra responsibilities and tasks that have built up around the job over the years. Conversely, it may be that the post is no longer necessary for the organization – those tasks attached to it which do still have to be done could be carried out by other departments more effectively.

The next stage (providing the organization still feels that it is necessary to fill the vacancy) is to draw up a description of the skills, demeanour and attributes that an employee would need to do the job effectively. One way is to use a checklist, such as Rodger's Seven-Point Plan, which sets out a series of headings, under which the manager should list the requirements to do the job. The plan covers:

1 Physique, manner and bearing.
2 Attainments – education,
                  – experience.
3 General intelligence.
4 Special aptitudes.
5 Interests.
6 Disposition.
7 Circumstances.

This person/job profile can then be used to form the basis of a vacancy advertisement. Consideration should be given to the most suitable and cost-effective ways of advertising for job applicants. Some businesses, e.g. publishing, journalism and TV/radio, receive and recruit from on-spec applications. Other vacancies are advertised in trade magazines, in local and national newspapers, in job centres, and in university and college careers offices – depending upon the type of job and the type of candidate required.

10.3 Selection

Selection follows recruitment. Having located possible applicants and attracted them to the organization, the company has to select the most appropriate applicants, turn them into candidates and persuade them that it is in their interests to join the company. It must be remembered that, even when there is high unemployment, selection is a two-way process, with the candidates assessing the company just as much as the company assessing them.

Selection techniques

Several techniques are used in the selection process. These include the following.

Application forms

The information contained within an application form or letter received from an applicant constitutes the basis of the selection process. This form provides evidence of the candidate's suitability or unsuitability for a particular post. If the application form reveals that the candidate is suitable, then he/she can be called for an interview. Often an organization will require an applicant to use a standard application form designed by the company, so as to make him/her address areas of character, competence, experience, etc. which the organization wishes to know about.

Interviews

The interview is the most common selection technique. Conducting an effective interview requires good preparation, so that the interviewer is confident conducting the interview. This will enable him/her to exploit to the full the information already provided by the candidate in the application form, and to maintain control of the interview.

This last point is important. The interviewer needs to make sure the questions are answered fully, and that the interviewee does not escape with half or unsatisfactory answers. The interviewer needs to cut short responses which go on too long, and also to resist the temptation to get sidetracked by an issue the interviewee has raised – no matter how interesting!

The interviewer has more chance of maintaining control in the interview if he/she allocates time for dealing with particular areas and sticks to that time schedule. Control is lost if the interviewees succeed in dominating the conversation with their own interests, if they are allowed to spend as much time as they choose over an answer, or if they are allowed to interrupt the interviewer continually.

Types of interview questions

Questioning plays a vital part in a selection interview, as it is the primary means by which information is obtained and the candidate's suitability for the post judged. Questions can either be closed or open ones. Closed questions require a specific yes or no reply, and should be used to check information already provided by the candidate or to change the direction of the interview. Open questions require some reflection or elaboration upon a particular point. These are often used once the interview has been got under way by means of closed questions, and have the objective of getting the candidate to demonstrate his/her knowledge and skills to the interviewer.

Numbers of interviewers

Interviews are usually conducted on a one-to-one basis, but a two-to-one situation is also often used. The latter has the advantage of allowing one interviewer to observe the candidate's reactions while the other interviewer actually asks the questions. A slight disadvantage is that the candidate may be less forthcoming with more than one person present. Another form of interview is the panel interview, in which the candidate is faced with several interviewers. Often candidates are shown round the company, usually either by a fairly recently joined employee or by someone who would be working with the successful recruit. It is in this more relaxed situation that far more can often be learned about the candidates and their suitability for the job than in the selection interview proper.

Psychological tests

Psychological tests are standardized tests designed to provide a relatively objective measure of certain human characteristics, by sampling human behaviour. There are four categories of such tests:

1 *Intelligence tests*. These are designed to measure thinking abilities, i.e. verbal ability, spatial ability, and numerical ability. Popular tests used by personnel managers for selection purposes usually consist of several different sections, each of which aims to test the candidates in these ability areas.
2 *Aptitude tests*. These are tests of innate skills and are devised to obtain information about such skills as mechanical ability, logic and numerical ability, and manual dexterity.
3 *Attainment tests*. These measure the candidate's depth of knowledge or grasp of skills which have been learned in the past – usually at school or college. The tests therefore measure such skills as typing standards, spelling ability, and mental arithmetic.

4   *Personality tests*. These tests, although sometimes used in the selection process, are of limited value because of problems with their validity.

Psychological tests are not a basic part of the selection process, but they can provide useful additional information about a candidate, supplementing that obtained from application forms and interviews. They are particularly useful where objective information is needed, e.g. in assessing a candidate's suitability for computer programming training.

10.4 Training and development

Personnel management is also concerned with the training needs and the development of all the organization's employees. Companies which train their workforces tend to have significant competitive advantages over those companies which do not have training programmes, especially when skilled workers are in short supply.

The first requirement of a training programme is to establish what the training and development needs of the organization as a whole (and of individual personnel) are. Only after this has been done can plans be made with regard to the training required to meet those needs. This will include deciding on the objectives, content and methods of training to be used.

Benefits of training programmes

The implementation of a systematic training programme has a number of benefits. It provides a pool of skilled manpower for the organization, it improves the existing skills in the company, it increases the knowledge and experience of employees, and it helps improve job performance and, consequently, productivity. Further benefits include an improved service to customers, greater commitment on the part of staff to the organization, and an increase in value of individual employees' knowledge and skills, together with personal growth opportunities for staff.

The Peter Principle

Continued training throughout a person's career is essential if the Peter Principle is to be avoided. This states that 'in a hierarchy every employee tends to rise to his level of incompetence'. (This applies to all organizations, not just to hierarchies.) The principle works on the basis that organizations want high performance, and so if a person is good at his job, he will be promoted to a better and more demanding one. Eventually he will reach a post which is beyond his abilities, and will be promoted no further. Peter's corollary is that 'in time, every post tends to be occupied by an employee who is incompetent to carry out its duties'. The work of the organization is done by those who have not yet reached their level of incompetence.

Identification of training needs

A training need arises when there is a shortfall in terms of employee knowledge, understanding, skill and attitudes compared with what is required by the job, or by the demands of organizational change. This can be expressed by Figure 10.1 (G. A. Cole, 1983).

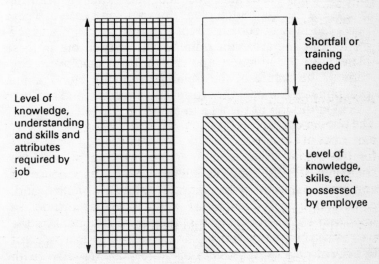

Level of knowledge, understanding and skills and attributes required by job

Shortfall or training needed

Level of knowledge, skills, etc. possessed by employee

Figure 10.1   Identification of training need

Different jobs will demand different things of people. Some will require little knowledge of the work necessary and little skill, but perhaps an aptitude which gives attention to detail. Other jobs will demand specialist knowledge, an understanding of the concepts behind the job, and a high level of specialist skill.

Information for training

Data for analysing training needs can be gained at three levels:

1 *Organizational level*. Here data about the organization as a whole are gathered, e.g. its structure, markets, products or services.
2 *Job level*. Data at this level concern jobs and activities, e.g. job descriptions, personnel specifications, etc.
3 *Individual level*. This level of data is concerned with appraisal records, personal training records, test results, etc.

Training programmes

Once training needs have been identified, training priorities can be sorted, and initial plans drawn up and costed. These plans can then be submitted for approval to senior management. The key areas for training will be spelt out in these plans, also the numbers and categories of employees concerned, the nature of the training proposed, etc. Training programmes can be either formal or informal, and can take place on-the-job or through in-house or day-release courses in local colleges.

Evaluation of training programmes

Evaluation is part of the control process of these training programmes. The aim is to obtain feedback about the results or outputs of the training, and then to use this feedback to assess the value and success of the particular training methods used, with a view to improvement where it seems necessary.

10.5 Personnel management and employment legislation

A person employed by an organization is either employed under a contract of service, as an employee, or under a contract for services, as an independent contractor. It is only the former which is referred to as a contract of employment.

It is important to distinguish whether a person is under a contract of employment or not. If a person is under that contract and is therefore an employee, his/her employer is liable vicariously for any civil wrongs the employee may commit in the course of his/her work; whereas an employer bears no such responsibility in respect of independent contractors. In addition, only employees are granted certain rights, or protection and benefits.

Duties of employers and employees

Both employers and employees have certain duties to one another under common law. Thus the employer is obliged to pay wages, provide work, take reasonable care of the employee, indemnify the employee for any expenses and liabilities, and treat the employee with courtesy. The employee is obliged to render a personal service, take care in the performance of his/her duties, obey reasonable instructions from the employer, act in good faith towards the employer, and not impede his/her employer's business.

Employment protection rights

The personnel manager has to be aware of the legislation protecting the rights of employees, because it is part of his job to make sure such legislation is complied with.

The Employment Protection (Consolidation) Act 1978 gives employees protection over a wide variety of matters, including:

1 Maternity pay and leave.
2 Ante-natal care.
3 Guarantee payment.
4 Time off for a variety of activities, including duties as a

Justice of the Peace, trade union duties, and for job-seeking.

The Act also gives every employee the right not to be unfairly dismissed by his/her employer. Two points must be noted here:

(*a*)   The burden of proving that there was a dismissal rests with the employee.

(*b*)   The burden of proving the reasons for the dismissal is on the employer.

Dismissal is defined as including the following:

1   Termination of the contract by the employer with or without notice.
2   Expiry of a fixed-term contract without renewal.
3   Termination of the contract by the employee with or without notice in circumstances such that he/she is entitled to terminate it without notice due to the conduct of the employer.

Dismissal can be deemed to be fair in the following circumstances:

(*a*)   If the employee is proving incapable of, or unqualified in, his work.

(*b*)   Redundancy of the employee, although an employee unfairly selected for redundancy will be regarded as unfairly dismissed.

(*c*)   Misconduct.

(*d*)   Where the employee could not continue in his/her job without causing him/herself or employer to contravene the law.

Part of the Employment Protection (Consolidation) Act provides for industrial tribunals. The jurisdiction of industrial tribunals extends from claims for unfair dismissal, and complaints relating to maternity provisions, to questions of equal opportunity and to unfair discrimination on grounds of race.

10.6 Summary

1 Personnel management can be regarded as one part of the general processes of management, and as such not exclusively the job of the personnel department and manager. In many small companies there will not be a separate personnel department.

2 Many of the duties undertaken by personnel managers also impinge on general management, such as organizing people at work, motivating them and encouraging good relations between staff and management, and sometimes training and development (especially on-the-job training and learning by others' example, and through the delegation of responsibility).

3 The aim of recruitment is to try to attract potential new employees to apply for jobs advertised by the company. During selection, the company tries to identify those applicants who will meet the organization's needs, both in the short and in the longer term.

4 External applicants are usually selected on the basis of an initial application form and by interviews. Psychological tests are also used sometimes to assess either the level of skills a candidate already has, or inherent skills.

5 The company will have far more information about the suitability of internal applicants for posts than for outsiders. In these cases interviews should not be the main basis of judgement.

10.7 Quick questions

1 What are the key areas of personnel management?
2 Differentiate between recruitment and selection procedures.
3 How can the use of psychological tests help in the selection process?
4 What are the benefits to a company of having a systematic programme of training for its employees?
5 Under what circumstances may an employee be fairly dismissed?

11
Management information systems

11.1 Introduction

Management information systems is a much discussed subject. MIS evolved as an extension of management accounting, using ideas and techniques in the area of management service, decision theory and behavioural theories of management. Management information systems have developed much in the last two decades mainly due to the introduction and development of computers which have revolutionized the processing of data.

The emphasis on this study of management information systems is not on the details or its make-up and operation but on the role and importance of the system for management and on how it itself is managed.

Management information systems are information systems using formal procedures to provide management at all levels, in all the functions of the business, with relevant information, both internal and external, so that decisions can be made which are timely and effective, enabling the planning, control and direction of the business to take place. A management information system has been defined as 'a system in which defined data are collected, processed and communicated to assist those responsible for the use of resources.'

As we study management information systems we will be concerned primarily with computer data based systems. It is important to note and remember, however, that the MIS concept predates computers. Essentially MIS evolved as an extension of management accounting, using ideas and techniques in the area of management service, decision theory and behavioural theories of management. However, the capabilities of computers have undoubtedly added to the development of the MIS concept. Now a management information system is most often a formalized, computer-based system able to integrate data from various sources to provide information for all levels of management planning, decision making and control within an organization. Thus the data processing system supports management information systems. Much of the information which the MIS uses is initially captured and stored by the data processing systems – which we shall examine later. Data processing and MIS are not the same however; data processing is oriented towards the capture, processing and storage of data whereas MIS is oriented towards using that data to produce management information.

It must be noted that an MIS is not a monolithic entity, but, rather, it is a federation of functional information systems. Specialists within each of the functions, such as finance, production, engineering, marketing, etc., are much more familiar with the information requirements of that function than anyone else in the organization. These specialists can design systems to produce the information required to manage their functions. These functional information systems interact with one another and often share the same data. The important point to remember is that these integrated functional information systems are the MIS.

Data is the central resource of an MIS and the management of this resource is crucial. The integration of these functional systems is dependent upon a data base management system – DBMS. A database management system is a program that serves as an interface between applications programs and a set of co-ordinated and integrated files called a database. The DBMS allows the various functional systems to access the same data, and can pool together related data from different files. It can be said, therefore, that the DBMS is perhaps the most important tool in making an MIS possible.

The manager's need for information

The construction and instalment of a management information system presupposes the need for information on the part of the manager.

On a general level it is evident that industrial organizations and their management will need increasing information in the future, for a number of reasons. First, development in technology, inflation, the influence of governments and other international agencies and the increasing size of organizations reflect, and have created, an increasingly complex business environment. Consequently the modern manager has to consider many more factors than his predecessor and hence his demand for information is correspondingly higher. Second, management science has developed considerably using a number of mathematical techniques which are extremely complex and lengthy calculation processes. These only provide the manager with good answers when supplied with sufficient, accurate data relevant to the problem. Third, business is being inundated with demands for information from society in general.

The whole purpose of a management information system, as we have already noted, is to provide information for management. We need to focus on the information systems primarily as they relate to management. Thus if we are to understand the need for management information (and therefore MIS) we need to briefly look at what management involves.

All managers must perform certain basic functions in order to achieve the goals/objectives of the organization. The objectives pursued differ in each organization but the basic functions of management are common to all. These functions are planning, organizing, staffing and controlling, and here we can briefly explain what these functions involve.

Planning

Planning involves making decisions with regard to the selection of both short-run and long-run business strategies and goals; the development of policies and procedures which will help accomplish objectives; the establishment of operating standards which serve as the basis for control; and the revision of earlier plans in light of changing conditions. The planning function involves a number of steps as follows:

1   Identifying the objective. Information is needed to bring awareness of problems and opportunities.

2 Gathering and analysing facts.
3 Seeking suitable alternatives. The manager must seek out the most attractive possible course of action. It is the skill of the manager and the quality of information which he receives that determines the appropriateness of the options selected.
4 Evaluating and selecting alternative.
5 Follow-up.

Organizing

The organizing function involves the grouping of work teams into logical and efficient units in order to put plans into operation and achieve objectives. It has been defined as 'the grouping of activities necessary to accomplish goals and plans, the assignment of these activities to appropriate departments, and the provision for authority delegation and co-ordination.'

Staffing

The staffing function involves selecting people, training employees to meet their job requirements, preparing employees for promotion to positions of greater responsibility and reassigning or dismissing employees when necessary.

Controlling

Control is, in effect, the follow-up to planning, checking up on past and current performance to see if objectives are being achieved. The steps in the control function are as follows:

1 Setting standards. It can be noted here that the setting of realistic standards requires quality information.
2 Measuring actual performance. This step in the control function requires timely and accurate performance information.
3 Comparison of performance with set standards.
4 Taking control action. If the performance falls short of

standards, and those standards are realistic, then correcting action will need to be taken.

The performance and success of the business depends on how well these basic managerial functions are being carried out. The fundamental assumption usually made is that this is dependent, in part, upon how well the information needs of managers are being met. This is because each function involves decision-making and to make a good decision requires information as to the internal or external events that led to the need for a decision to be made; and the likely consequences of alternative decisions. Good information can lead to good decision-making which in turn leads to a successful attainment of organizational goals.

In considering the need for management information it is also evident that a common information need basic to all managers is an understanding of the purpose of the organization, i.e. its policies, programs, plans and goals. Thus the specific information needed by a particular manager includes everything that managers must have to do:

1 Establish, evaluate, and adjust goals.
2 Develop plans and standards and initiate action.
3 Measure actual performance and take appropriate action when performance varies from the standard.
4 Assess achievements.

The attributes of information required by managers for management

There is a distinctive managerial perspective on relevance, i.e. different managers view an organization in different ways and different managers may vary in their belief as to what information is relevant in analysing a problem and in decision-making. A management information system must be designed so that the manager is not faced with a scarcity of information yet guarding against the opposite situation of information overload. Management, given too much undigested information, will simply ignore it.

Information is a business resource, and like any other business resource it is not free. It is, therefore, necessary that the cost of acquiring the resource be compared with the value to be obtained from its availability. For example, the MIS designer must consider whether or not the revenue will be raised enough to justify additional costs which are frequently incurred to give managers more accurate, more timely, and more complete information with which to make decisions.

The kind of information wanted by managers from a management information system has the following attributes or characteristics:

1 *Accuracy*. Facts and information should be correct. Accuracy may be defined as the ratio of correct information to the total amount of information over a period of time.

2 *Timeliness*. The characteristic of timeliness is important since it is of little consolation to the manager to know that although the information was accurate, it arrived too late to be of use. Accuracy alone is not enough. In the past a trade-off between timeliness and accuracy was often required, i.e. greater accuracy might require more input data control points which could slow down the processing speed and therefore reduce the timeliness of the output information. Computer usage, however, reduces the significance of this conflict between accuracy and processing speed.

3 *Completeness*. For managers to make a good decision they require accurate, timely and complete information. All the necessary information is required otherwise a critical missing fact, vital to the decision, may result in a poor decision being made. A dramatic historical example of the consequence or failure to consolidate related pieces of information occurred at Pearl Harbor in 1941. If the data available had been integrated, the United States authorities would have been warned of the danger of a Japanese attack. Better integration of the facts available at scattered points in a business, for the purpose of furnishing managers with more complete information is a goal of information system designers.

4 *Conciseness*. A computer-based information system stores vast quantities of facts and data. Managers cannot hope to extract the information required from these mountains of printed material. Concise information

which summarizes the relevant data and which points out areas of exception to normal or planned activities is what is often needed by managers.

5   *Relevance*. Information that does not lead to action or provide new knowledge or understanding is irrelevant. In other words, information is relevant and is only worth producing if it will 'identify and support necessary action by responsible individuals within the organization'.

One of the reasons for the growth of computer based information systems is that traditional systems do not provide information with these five basic attributes. A computer-based management information system can be defined as a collection of inter-related computer-based processing procedures developed in an organization and integrated as necessary with other manual, mechanical, and/or electronic procedures for the purpose of providing accurate, timely, complete, concise and relevant information to aid decision-making and other managerial functions.

Information needs and MIS design

The information needs of managers which must be met by a management information system is complicated by the fact that there are a number of organizational levels of management. There are three organizational levels of management; top, middle and lower and concomitantly three types of management process; strategic, tactical and operational. The decision types and information characteristics vary between these different types of management; thus the MIS needs to provide information for day-to-day operations; information for tactical planning and decision-making; and information for the support of strategic planning and decision-making. In other words, one way of viewing information is to classify it in terms of the type of information provided to different managerial levels.

Higher levels of management tend to be planning-oriented and therefore need information relating more to the external environment, as well as internal data of a highly summarized nature. Lower levels of management deal with more detailed reports, generally control-oriented and relating to internal matters. Middle management are less concerned with detailed control and more with tactical planning, but nevertheless have a vital role in the management control process of a business. These categories, although not as distinct as we have perhaps implied, do need to be borne in mind when designing an MIS. The right amount of information must be available to support the appropriate level of management: too much can be as damaging as too little. Data must be distilled in order to produce the right quantity of information for each managerial level.

Figure 11.1 provides further explanation of how a management information system needs to be designed so as to provide appropriate information for each managerial level.

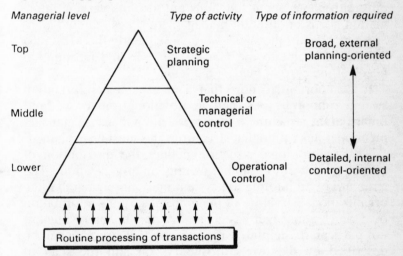

Figure 11.1

Each managerial level in the diagram relates to a different type of activity. These levels may be regarded as a pyramid with the bottom level providing information for the higher levels; the fourth level represents the pinnacle for which all information is filtered and summarized. Allied to each information level is the associated concept of information as the means of enabling the organization to control its activities or to ensure that it does not deviate from its plans.

Information needs and the design of an MIS to meet those needs is further complicated by the fact that management in different functions will also require different information. For example, product planners will require marketing and cost information as well as much external information; personnel management will require payroll, productivity and training information and production management will require detailed stock, machine breakdown and productivity information. It is evident that the types of decision made by managers vary so much and so the most fundamental requirement of a management information system is that it be sufficiently flexible to cope with the changing requests by management for information.

A management information system must be designed so that it will meet not only the information needs of different levels of management and the information needs of the different management functions but also the varying information needs of different management styles. No two managers manage in the same way; consequently the MIS must be able to adapt to the managerial style and information needs of the current managerial team.

It is important to note that a management information system cannot be designed in isolation from or without regard to the structure of the organization, because management operates within that structure. This must be explained.

An organizational structure defines the distribution of authority and responsibility within an organization. The structure of an information system must closely parallel the organizational structure of the entity it serves – information over which a manager has no control may be interesting but not particularly helpful. An organizational structure can be described by the levels of supervision and the span of control. The span of control describes the number of subordinates reporting to a superior.

Some organizations can be classified on the basis of their adaptation to the environment: mechanistic systems and organismic systems can be distinguished. Mechanistic organizations are often found in traditional industries where innovation is slow and where management control and information are based on elaborate rules and procedure, e.g. the steel industry. Organismic organizations have a rapid rate of innovation with a less structured and a more consultative style of management. The management information system in this environment must be designed to provide management control and information relevant to a relatively uncertain and unstructured situation.

Finally the type of technology available is a major determinant of managerial style – influencing the line of command and the span of control. Consequently the design of an MIS will be influenced to a significant extent by the type of technology within the organization.

11.2 The design function

Introduction

As, perhaps, we have already seen, the usefulness of an MIS for the manager and the management functions, is largely determined in the design stage. We have already examined the purpose of an MIS and the information needs that it must be able to meet and which therefore must be taken into account in its design. Now it is important that we gain some understanding of the design function and the components of an MIS. The management information system itself needs to be 'managed' and the design stage is important in the future management of the MIS; indeed it can be regarded as the first stage in the management of an MIS.

The systems development process

The four basic stages in the life cycle of a management information system are:

1 System definition and analysis.
2 System design.
3 System development and implementation.
4 System operation.

The responsibility for these elements of systems-work lies with the systems analyst and his team of systems people and the operating personnel. We need to look briefly and in general terms at these four basic stages and the role of the systems analyst before we go on to concentrate upon the essential components of a management information system.

The systems process commences with the definition of the problem. The systems analyst is rarely asked to find out if the problem exists. Usually, management becomes aware of a problem and asks the analyst to assess the existing system and propose ways of improving it. Much fact finding is necessary and many answers need to be obtained before a clear systems definition of the problem can be determined. This can be a lengthy and expensive stage in the systems process, but it is important to do it thoroughly for, after this stage, the analyst will be able to formulate clear objectives for the remainder of the project.

It is not necessary to discover all possible facts and information before beginning to define the objectives and the requirements of any proposed system. The experienced analyst will be able to sift the information and decide what is particularly relevant. He has to collect sufficient relevant data to enable him to define clearly the exact nature of the problem and to outline possible alternative systems that could be designed to overcome the problem. The fact-finding task involves personal consultations not only with top management but with managers of affected departments, the data-processing department, internal users of the system and possibly some external users such as customers who will be affected by any proposed changes.

Therefore, in his first report to management, the analyst will present a clear systems definition of the problem together with the outlines of some alternative systems with a qualitative assessment of their relative advantages and disadvantages. It is not for the analyst to decide which system should be adopted for further detailed investigation, although he can make recommendations and the way in which he presents his report can influence management in their decisions. From this, one or more alternative systems will be outlined from which one will be selected for detailed investigation and development.

Once systems selection has been made, an estimate of costs and benefits of the system must be carried out. The cost of the system has a significant bearing on its feasibility.

If the selected system is to be developed and implemented successfully the systems analyst will need the confidence and full support of everyone affected by the proposed system. All concerned must understand what is being proposed and appreciate how it will solve existing problems. The 'systems proposal' is a formal written document setting out the nature and scope of the proposed solution. It is studied by each party concerned, modified as required and eventually formally agreed to. Thereafter, it serves as a guideline for the duration of the project.

Once agreement has been reached on the systems proposal and authorization given for further development, the systems analyst can develop the actual mechanics for a workable system. This involves preparation of detailed specifications of computer programs, including details of inputs, outputs, data file structures, procedures for processing work and instructions for doing work. In effect, the design of a system involves the accomplishment of the following basic tasks:

1 Establishing output requirements
2 File design
3 Input requirements and format
4 Procedure design
5 Design and specification of controls.

Systems design is followed by program development. Ideally, the systems analyst has no involvement in actually writing and testing programs. His job is to provide additional information and clarify requirements if required by programmers, to establish a basis for testing the reliability and accuracy of programs as they are developed, and to maintain close contact with programming management to ensure that programs are developed in order and on time.

The final testing of the system as a whole is carried out during a period of parallel running: that is, all the procedures of the new system are carried out whilst the old system is still in operation giving a final opportunity to check user-reaction to the new system before the old one is superseded. This is the point at which the new system can be said to be fully implemented. Even after full implementation some problem may arise; therefore for a short period after implementation the systems analyst should be available to offer advice and to supervise any modifications that may be necessary to ensure the smooth operation of the system.

Figure 11.2 gives a clear overview of the system process from the problem definition to the completion.

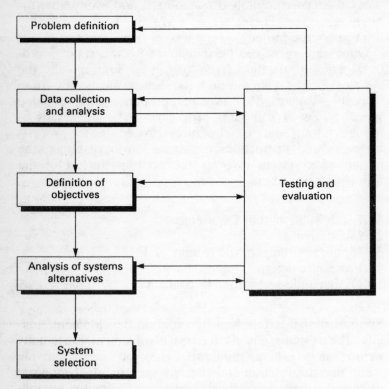

Figure 11.2   From problem definition to system selection

Data processing

The data processing system supports the management information system. Much of the information which the MIS uses is initially captured and stored by the data processing system. To contrast the two, data processing is oriented towards the capture, processing and storage of data, whereas MIS is oriented towards using that data to provide management information.

Data processing consists of three activities: input, manipulative and output activities. Input activities consist of organizing or capturing data in some form which is suitable for subsequent processing. Manipulative activities consist of up to four operations as follows:

1 *Classifying*: identifying and arranging items with like characteristics;
2 *Sorting*: the arrangement of data in a predetermined sequence to facilitate processing;
3 *Calculating*: arithmetic manipulation of data;
4 *Summarizing*: data must often be condensed, compressed or exceptions highlighted so that output reports may be of value by being concise and effective.

After input and manipulation of data, the final activity is output and interpretation of the results. The raw data having been captured and processed the results can be subject to a number of distinct operations including storage (filing), retrieval, and reproduction of the data as output reports. Finally, the output is interpreted and the resulting information communicated to management.

Databases and database management

Database can be understood to be two different things. Depending on the content it can refer to stored information or to the 'logical map' used to organize the way different records are stored and related to each other.

The database approach to information systems can offer solutions to many problems. By taking into account the variety of different needs and viewpoints of data users the database approach permits an open structure to the information rather than one which is too heavily weighted in favour of one particular user's needs.

The essential feature of a database approach is that data is regarded as a central resource of a company or organization. The intention is that data, like buildings, equipment, personnel or capital of the business, should be owned and maintained for the use and benefit of the organization as a whole. Due to the enormous technological advances in computer engineering in data capture, storage, processing and transmission, it is now practicable in many cases to record and store all the information generated by any operation or decision within a company in one of the set of storage files. The comprehensive data stored in this way will then be available to provide management with any information which may be required in the future. In other words, different programs can be written, each using the same large data 'bank' as a source for processing information. In this extreme form, all data is regarded as potentially useful and should be stored away for possible use in the future. In practice, only the data likely to be of use is captured, because the additional expense and effort involved in being completely comprehensive would be greater than the value of the extra data. This is the database concept.

The database concept and approach has four major objectives according to Everest (1974).

1   The database should be shared; in other words, different users with different applications should be capable of accessing the same actual data at the same time. This reduces the need for duplicate copies of data and saves storage space. It also ensures that the latest updates are available to all users of the data and that different incompatible versions do not evolve.
2   Integrity of the database. In a shared data environment, this objective is fundamental since multiple users have access to the same data. No one user can be allowed to make alterations to the data which would impair other applications.
3   The database management system must be responsive to an environment of diverse users, having diverse needs and requiring diverse modes of access.
4   A fourth and very important objective is evolvability, which is the ability of the database management system to develop and meet the needs of future applications which could not be anticipated at the initial design stage.

For an MIS to have long-term survival within a computerized data-processing environment, it must possess all the attributes listed in these four objectives. To achieve them the data must be defined and exist independently of the application programs that use it.

Data independence has two major elements (Everest, 1974). First, there is the separation of the logical definition of data in the database from the physical representation and storage of the data on the hardware discs etc., supporting the database. Second, there is program data independence by which we mean the separation of the logical definition of data as viewed by the user in his application program from the logical definition of the data in the database. This yields three different conceptual levels or views of the data. The definitions of these conceptual levels or data relationships are as follows:

Hierarchical structure

Data items are stored from the top downwards, each item being related to only one item above it in the hierarchy, but to any number of items below it. For example, if a large multinational company built up a database of all its branches throughout the world it might be structured as shown in Figure 11.3.

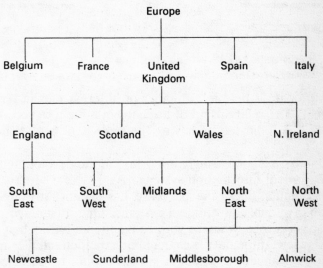

Figure 11.3

Network structure

This is similar to a hierarchical structure but any data item may be related to any number of other data items. For example, a database detailing a sales system might be structured as shown in Figure 11.4.

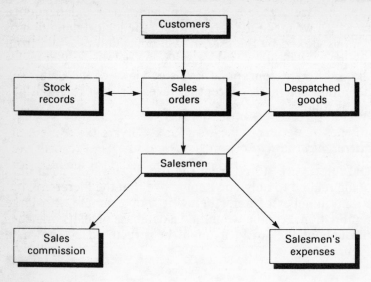

Figure 11.4

Relational structure

All the data is held in a number of different files in record format. The relationship of a record in a file to a record in another is indicated by having the same data field value in each.

Database is increasingly important in the development of management information systems. As a system of structuring computer files, the database has significantly greater flexibility than conventional systems. One advantage of a database is that, whereas with conventional files, when one user's view of the data is changed or extended, all files must also be changed, a database system should be sufficiently flexible to be capable of enhancement for one user without affecting its use by others.

It is also important to remember that the database is dynamic: not only do the data items themselves change, but the types of data and the relationships between the items will also change. In addition to the database, software will be required to handle the data. Such software is called the 'database management system' or DBMS.

Database management systems

We have already noted much earlier that the database management system (DBMS) is perhaps the most important tool in making a management information system possible. The DBMS is software packages which are used to manage the large and complex file structures which make up the database. Each DBMS works on a particular logical data structure, i.e. it organizes its records in a certain way. It provides all necessary facilities for specifying the content of records and the way in which different types of records are inter-related. It also provides all the technical facilities for ensuring data integrity, etc. The DBMSs make databases available to a large number of users. The users of the databases do not directly access the database. Instead they access the DBMS which interprets the data requirements into accesses to the database, makes the accesses required, and returns the results to the user in the form that the user requires.

Many of the better DBMSs provide a number of ways of access. This is good because there are many types of user. Users can be untrained and intermittent in their use of the management information system. These 'casual users' should not be required to be familiar with the system and usually do not want to be trained in its use. They should be encouraged by its ease of use.

When changes are made in the database the DBMS automatically re-indexes records and provides the interface with the application programs which transfer the input and output to and from the database. The application programs should be independent, as far as possible, of the actual organization of the database. The DBMS has to protect data from unauthorized access and from corruption during processing. By keeping a record of data items accessed, the DBMS can identify redundant items that can be removed from the database.

Management information systems – the problems

We can identify a number of problems which are associated with or arise out of management information systems.

It is evident that most MISs are designed on the assump-

tion that the critical deficiency under which managers operate is a lack of relevant information. Yet the manager's
information problem is primarily one of an overabundance
of irrelevant information. There is a real difference here.
The consequences of changing the emphasis of an MIS from
supplying relevant information to eliminating irrelevant
information are considerable. If the preoccupation is with
supplying relevant information, attention is almost exclusively given to the generation, storage and retrieval of
information. If, on the other hand, one sees the manager's
information problem primarily, but not exclusively, as one
that arises out of an overabundance of irrelevant information, then the two most important functions of an information system become filtration (or evaluation) and
condensation.

Most designers of management information systems
'determine' what information is needed by asking the managers what information they would like to have. This is
based on the assumption that managers know what information they need and want it. For a manager to know what
information he needs he must be aware of each type of
decision he should make and he must have an adequate
model of each. These conditions, however, are seldom
satisfied. In short, one cannot specify what information is
required for decision-making until an explanatory model of
the decision process and the system involved has been
constructed and tested.

Second, it is evident that most designers of management
information systems seek to make their systems as innocu-
ous and unobtrusive as possible to managers lest they
become frightened by the system. The designers try to
provide managers with a very easy access to the system and
assure them that they need to know nothing more about it.
This, however, leaves managers unable to evaluate the MIS
as a whole. In failing to evaluate their MIS, managers
delegate much of the control of the organization to the
system's designers and operators who may have many
qualities but who are rarely competent in managerial skills.
It can be said that, in order to avoid this problem, no
management information system should ever be installed
unless the managers for whom it is intended are trained to

evaluate and hence control it rather than be controlled by it themselves.

We can identify further problems arising from management information systems in the area of database management. Common data in a database can imply centralized storage, but this may conflict with the company's needs. Database access can be distributed to satellite computers and remote terminals. The database itself can also be distributed but the costs of data communications are high and must be carefully assessed; consistency is complicated by the unreliability of communication lines.

There are also real problems of privacy and security of data. Much can be done to protect the security and reliability of data, but users and managers should question the assumptions built into the database. Another problem is that of recovery of data. Since the data is held only once and its use is widespread, the problem of recovery in the event of system failure is one of the most crucial. Database management software is therefore constantly being improved in terms of recovery capability.

We mentioned above the unreliability of communication lines; it is evident that communication problems may exist within a management information system. These may arise on three different levels; the technical, the semantic and the effectiveness levels. Effectiveness is perhaps the major problem area within a management information system.

'Effectiveness' implies a relationship to purpose. The effectiveness of a communication refers to the changes it causes in the pursuit of a purpose. The effectiveness of a communication is determined by comparing the purposeful states of the decision-maker before and after receipt of the communication. The communication is considered to have been effective if it changes a purposeful state in one of three possible ways:

1 Informs; changes the probabilities of a choice.
2 Instructs; changes the efficiencies of a course of action.
3 Motivates; changes the values of the outcomes.

Effective communication of information may result from proper sequencing, spacing, colouring, etc., all of which affect or result in the reduction of uncertainty in the decision-maker.

We can also argue that a management information system can suffer from problems associated with organizational structure. The four most prominent problems of modern organizations are:

1 Rigidity. Organizations tend to resist change.
2 Information failures. Failures in communication may occur between organizational sub-units due to their physical separation and specialization of functions.
3 Suboptimisation. This refers to the problem whereby an organizational sub-unit, by attempting to optimize its assigned subgoal, makes it more difficult for the organization as a whole to achieve its global goal.
4 Individual motivation. Where there is an area of conflict between individual goals and organizational goals.

The problem, encountered by management information systems, of encouraging the flow of consistent, accurate and relevant information to the top of the hierarchy is difficult. For example, reports which are summarized from a number of departments in the hierarchy may be based on different timescales, different assumptions, different interpretations of rules, etc. Such problems have led the NCC (the UK National Computing Centre) to state: 'Hierarchical structures tend to encourage formal, highly structural information flows in which information is inconsistent, incomplete and filtered (possibly in the wrong way).'

This view is supported by the problem of empire-building which leads to a duplication of effort and information. For instance, a lack of trust or an unappropriate organizational structure may cause both the sales department and the production department to maintain records of customers orders.

It can be noted that another problem of management information systems lies in people's acceptance and use of these systems – certainly during the development period and when they are first implemented. Employees can often regard a management information system in a negative way. They may think that their jobs will be less secure, that they might lose the independence that they previously enjoyed, that their relationships with others will change for the worse, and that their work will change. Some of these can be positive changes for the staff, but they may be perceived as negative. Unless steps are taken, during the development of the MIS and when it is implemented, to ensure that the people are fully informed about it, there is no reason to assume that they will co-operate.

It is important to communicate to the manager not only the political advantages of the information systems approach, of relevant, timely, accurate, understandable, and up-to-date information which is provided to the correct level of detail, highlighting critical factors which control the firm's success, but of potential pitfalls that should be avoided. For example, more information is not necessarily better: it may be too detailed for 'digestion' or irrelevant to the decision-maker. Decision making will not necessarily improve because the information is available: it may be ignored as many managers will prefer to keep to the combination of intuition, experience and judgement to make decisions. There should be wide discussion within the organization of these aspects so that management is aware of the pitfalls.

11.3 Managing the management information system

Structure of the MIS function

Typically, the MIS function is located in one of two areas in an organization. The chief MIS executive may be reporting to the vice-chairman and controller or reporting directly to the chairman as vice-chairman of MIS.

Figure 11.5 illustrates this:

Being the chief accounting officer in a corporation, the controller was looked upon as the primary provider of quantitative management information. In addition, functions in the controller's area such as payroll, accounts payable etc., were often the first applications to be computerized. Therefore, the information systems function often originated and matured with the controller's organization. The primary disadvantage of the chief MIS executive reporting to the controller is that the computer resource may be dominated and used primarily to solve problems with the controller's area, leaving other functions neglected. The

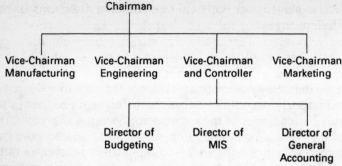

Figure 11.5

primary advantage of the chief MIS executive reporting to the controller is that accounting is an information oriented discipline, and accountants are well-trained in the area of control.

Many of the larger, more mature management information systems organizations are separate from any one function, and have a chief MIS executive, who is a vice-chairman, reporting directly to the Chairman. This location for the MIS function helps to ensure that each of the functional areas will receive the unbiased attention of the MIS department.

Organization of the MIS function varies from firm to firm, particularly between small and large firms, but there are five distinct functions that must be carried out within the MIS department.

First, the systems software group installs and maintains systems software such as operating systems and database management systems. These are technical and highly skilled programmers.

Second, applications software is developed, or selected and purchased, by systems and programming.

Third, the technical support staff is in charge of hardware maintenance and establishing data processing standards.

Fourth, the data processing operations department manages the day-to-day operations of the computer hardware and the processing of computer jobs.

Fifth, a function that is relatively new in most larger MIS organizations is that of the database administrator (DBA). The DBA is responsible for co-ordinating the database including provisions for data security.

We can focus on the final two areas or functions of the MIS department.

Management of data processing

Managing data processing operations is much like the management of any other function within an organization. Management must be concerned with maintaining sufficient capacity to process computer jobs. Users of the resource should be charged for resources they use. Personnel must be hired, managed, and, if necessary, dismissed, and machines must be maintained in operable conditions.

Processing capacity may be limited by any number of factors, including primary storage size, secondary storage size, etc. Any of these factors can be a bottleneck that limits the capacity of the computer system. Data processing management must monitor these resources and determine if one is likely to become a bottleneck in the future.

The database administrator

The role of the database administrator (DBA) is crucial to the success of the database and the management information system. The DBA could be said to be the manager of the database – he is responsible for ensuring that the required levels of privacy, security and integrity of the database are maintained.

One of the main objectives of the database approach is to facilitate the sharing of data between many users. Users may, however, resist both the DBA taking control of 'their' data and other users having access to it. This may lead to conflict. There needs to be a DBA with the necessary status to apply a corporation-wide perspective to mediate in such a conflict.

There are a number of problems that may arise from the sharing of data. The balancing of conflicting interests requires a managerial perspective and a good knowledge of the business. Other problems require technical knowledge. The DBA will have to deal with complaints about the usage of the database and to provide technical training.

In practice, the DBA function needs to be carried out by a team. The director of this team needs to have sufficient standing in the organization to remain independent of 'pressure groups' of database users. The DBA is expected to be a good communicator and has to discuss aspects of data use and storage with other managers, user staff, operations staff and application developers. It could be said that part of the DBA's role is that of 'public relations officer' for the database.

The DBA must perform a basic managerial function in that he must plan ahead. The logical data structures will need to be changed over time according to the changing needs of users. The DBA must be aware of present and future needs and be aware of any advances in the hardware and software. The DBA must also assess the performance of the database. In this the DBA may aim towards 'satisficing' on a wide range of criteria, rather than optimise on any one criterion, in other words ensure that the performance of the database on a wide range of issues is satisfactory.

The position of the DBA in the organization

In some organizations the DBA function is seen as separate from the Data Processing Department. Such an arrangement is certainly desirable in view of the managerial aspects of the role; the DBA function should not be perceived as purely the concern of the technical and computer area.

More commonly the DBA function is carried out as part of the Data Processing Department or Management Services Department. In this case the DBA is often given managerial responsibilities without the status to carry them out.

It must be noted that a distinction may be made between the database administrators who are mainly responsible for the efficient running of the database and are members of the Data Processing Department and the data administrators, placed at corporate management level, who are responsible for the development and co-ordination of the policies and procedures of the 'data resource of the organization'. This distinction, once rarely found, is now a feature of a number of MIS organizations with large databases.

Managing the operation of management information systems

The MIS is a complex, valuable resource. It should be subject to the same kinds of management controls devoted to other important company resources. Two important management controls of MIS include first, an information system master plan, and second, the segregation of functions.

Information system master plan

The information system master plan should outline overall strategy for implementing the system. This plan should include major components of the system and interfaces among them. A good plan lists the order in which each component should first be implemented as well as implementation dates. Such a plan clarifies objectives and provides a sense of ordered progress to the development of the information system. Without a master plan the information system is likely to become a hotch-potch of incompatible computer programs.

Segregation of functions

A cardinal principle of good internal control – which is a primary function of management – is the segregation of functions. The EDP department should be segregated from users and should have control over the data and program files. However it should never have the authority to originate inputs or correct errors in them, unless the errors themselves originate in the EDP.

Functions within the EDP department should also be segregated. It is most important to segregate the duties of systems and programming personnel from the duties of equipment personnel and operators. To maintain effective control over EDP operations standard procedures must be established.

11.4 Further reflections

In the foregoing section we have concentrated our thoughts upon a centralized Management Information System; all users accessing and receiving their particular processed management reports from the data base management system. From this we may identify a number of benefits:

1   The staff are able to specialize and develop a professional approach to computing.
2   It facilitates control of the database on a corporate level whereby the organization is able to determine what data is captured and maintain its integrity and security.
3   It facilitates technical competence and research.
4   A comparative cost advantage is gained; an economy of scale may well exist in the operation of the MIS system.

We noted in the introduction to the chapter the fact that MIS predated the computer. It may also be noted that the MIS need not be centralized. The benefits of a decentralized MIS can be identified as follows:

1   It provides the availability of low-cost technology.
2   It avoids a backlog of work. An MIS operating on an organization wide basis has more work to deal with and may often accumulate a backlog whereas an MIS operating on a departmental or functional basis can undertake its own development projects.
3   A decentralized MIS will give experience in its use to more staff.
4   Having one's own system creates a more positive attitude amongst users.

The future of MIS

The future of MIS maybe lies in a new discipline as information resources management (IRM). This includes the related activities of data processing, data communications and office automation. These three fields are interdependent as Figure 11.6 illustrates. The aim of IRM will be to deal with a number of problems arising out of the operation of an MIS as follows:

1   Maintaining a human perspective in an automated office
2   Maintaining job satisfaction
3   Changing managerial outlook to one of long-term strategic planning
4   Ensuring automated office systems are user orientated and that computer files are available to all users.

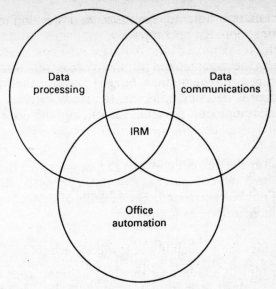

Figure 11.6 Information resources management

IRM will be facilitated by a new generation of computer with greater memory capacities, faster processing speeds, varied input and output, graphics, easier access, etc.

11.5 Summary

The information needs of the manager were considered in the design of the MIS. It was shown that the management information system must be designed to meet the information needs of management. This, it was noted, is complicated by the fact that there are three organizational levels of management – top management, making strategic decisions, middle management, which is primarily concerned with tactical planning, and lower management, concerned with operations and control. Complications arise out of the fact that different functions of management will require different information. Furthermore, it was noted that the MIS must be designed to meet the information needs of different styles of management.

It was also noted that it is important to take into consideration the organization structure when designing a management information system because of the simple fact that the management of the organization operates within that structure.

The next section looked at the design function itself because it is in this stage that the usefulness of the MIS for the manager is determined. First, the study focused on the systems development process, identifying the four basic stages:

1   System definition and analysis
2   System design
3   System development and implementation
4   System operation.

The final section of the study concentrated on managing the MIS. The text examined the structure of the MIS function, the management of data processing, and the role of the database administrator in managing the MIS. The role of the DBA was said to be crucial to the MIS.

11.6 Quick questions

1   Define and describe a management information system.
2   Why does a manager need information? Outline the attributes of this information.
3   Define and briefly describe a database and explain the importance of a DBMS for the MIS.
4   Describe the role of the DBA in managing the MIS, and identify the two management controls of an MIS.

12
Conclusions – successful management

This concluding chapter draws together some of the themes of the previous ones, and looks at how management success can be judged, measured and developed. A final section touches on some of the special problems associated with managing small businesses.

12.1 Introduction

As we have seen in the previous chapters, management is about planning (both on a day-to-day basis and on a longer, more strategic time span), and about organizing all the available resources to achieve these plans. It is about leading, co-ordinating, and motivating people, and controlling all the processes in the organization to meet the firm's stated objectives.

In order to do all this, managers have to be able to look ahead and assess the future realistically, to have imagination, and be able to make decisions based on sound understanding and judgement of the available data. Managers also have to be able to communicate effectively with their subordinates, superiors and peers, and to motivate, inspire and guide their staff so that everyone works together to achieve the organization's set goals and targets.

12.2 Management success

The acid test of management, ultimately, is business performance. A company can only justify its continued existence by the systematic making of profits. It is the responsibility of its managers to see that profits are made, and that the company produces products that consumers are willing to pay for. Other results of management, such as a happy and contented workforce and efficient communications, are good in themselves, but if they are not utilized to produce economic results as well, then the management can be deemed to be not very successful. The most effective manager is the one who is concerned with both people and production – the team manager on Blake and Mouton's managerial grid.

Effective management

A manager's effectiveness should be measured by what he/she achieves, not merely by what is done. Reddin (in *Managerial Effectiveness*) contrasts efficiency with effectiveness. An efficient manager does things right rather than doing the right things, he solves problems rather than producing new alternatives, he safeguards the company's resources instead of optimizing their utilization, he follows his set duties rather than obtaining new results, and he concentrates upon lowering costs instead of increasing profits.

Measuring management effectiveness

Appraising how well a manager does his job is very difficult – not least because of the problems of deciding what should be assessed, and then of deciding how the assessment should be done. Unlike a shop-floor worker, a manager cannot be judged on how well he does his job by the number of components he produces in any given period.

Traditional management appraisal tends to comprise a manager's immediate superior assessing and rating his performance, often using such unmeasurable criteria as 'motivation' and 'initiative'. Evaluation should be based upon how well the manager does his job and achieves results rather than upon his personality.

12.3 Management appraisal and development

Management appraisals on a regular basis allow managers to keep a check on both their own and their subordinate managers' performance, and to identify any areas of training needed. Such appraisals can also be used to review pay levels and to see if subordinates are suitable for promotion just yet or not.

To be most helpful all round, the appraisals should be carried out jointly, between the manager and his/her boss, preferably with any action on the manager's part to help improve his/her managerial performance agreed upon. Managerial assessments, as with any assessments, should *always* be as constructive, and as objective as possible.

Performance reviews

Campbell, Dunnett, Lawler and Weick (1970) define performance as 'behaviour that has been evaluated'. Therefore behaviour has to be observable and measurable to be part of any performance review. They go on to define effective managerial job behaviour as 'any set of managerial actions believed to be optimal for identifying, assimilating, and utilising both internal and external resources towards sustaining, over the long term, the functioning of the organizational unit for which a manager has some degree of responsibility'.

Measurement systems

Any system of measurement has to be based upon how well the manager carries out the functions of management, such as planning and control. It should consider all aspects of his behaviour in doing this, and it should not judge a manager on results and circumstances which are not his responsibility and are beyond his control.

Critical incidents method

This technique was developed by Flanagan in 1954. It consists of those people who are familiar with the particular job identifying the different behaviours which contribute towards doing the job well and effectively, and those with doing it ineffectively and badly. This gives a very practical index against which a manager's behaviour in the job can be compared and measured.

Planned performance programming

This is similar to management by objectives in that certain tasks are agreed upon and set by the manager concerned and his superior, and his effectiveness is judged by his achievement of these tasks.

Two other systems of measurement which are often used, but which do have problems attached to them, are global measures and objective measures.

Global measures

There are several different global measurement systems, as follows:

1 *Rankings* given by the manager's superiors for his effectiveness as a manager. This system is based on many different aspects of his behaviour, and it does have the advantage that he is compared to peers in similar situations. However, personal likes and dislikes on the part of the superior could influence the assessment, and it is difficult to tell if it is based on information which is relevant to the job or not.

2 *Salary and organizational level indices*. These are retrospective measures of performance, based on the idea that if a manager has reached a certain grade of position and salary, he must be doing his job well. This approach does have the problem that it does not allow for chance or luck playing a part in determining a manager's position in the organization. It is also a fairly circular idea, because often a favourable management appraisal leads to a salary increase.

Objective measures

These cover areas such as job attitude surveys among the manager's subordinates, absence rates among the workers, quantity and quality of output, etc. Although these measure job performance rather than personality, they often include factors which are not under the direct control of the manager, and they also tend to look at only one aspect of the manager's job.

The use of management appraisal

Like staff appraisal, management appraisal is very important in seeing where managers are perhaps having problems in certain aspects of their job. Where these are spotted, remedial action can be taken before it becomes too serious. It can also be very valuable in assessing how effective any management training has been. Good systems of appraisal will also give the managers guidelines for action and targets of performance to aim at.

Management training and education

Management training is normally used to improve the performance of the manager in his present job. Often a distinction is made between this training and management education, which is aimed more at high-flying promotion hopefuls. However, really all management training should be aiming to develop managers, not just in their present jobs, but to take on more responsibility in the future.

Owing to the increasing emphasis being placed upon management training and development, both at the outset of managers' careers and throughout their working lives, by such bodies as the British Institute of Management, job performance-based appraisal will probably become more and more common. Good management training has become and more important, because it has been seen and acknowledged that managers need wider and up-to-date skills, in order to react faster and to be more adaptable in the rapidly changing business environment.

12.4 Small business management

Small and medium-sized businesses pose special problems for their managers, although of course they do also have their own advantages over the management of larger organizations. Storey (1982) provides a working definition of a small business: a business with a small market share, which is normally managed by its owners. It makes or supplies a single product, or a small group of closely related products.

In a smaller company the managers have to be far less

specialized than in larger businesses. Their jobs will be far more varied, and cover a lot more of the business, and therefore they have to be flexible in their attitudes, open to change and innovation.

The business skills needed by an entrepreneur to start a business and build it up are very different from those needed to consolidate the company's growth. Once a business expands, the entrepreneur has to recognize that his former business practices and function, e.g. running everything himself, and taking all decisions, will have to change; otherwise the business is unlikely to survive in the long run.

Selected bibliography

Adams, J. S. (1963), 'Wage inequalities, productivity and quality', *Industrial Relations*, vol. 3, pp. 261–75.

Argenti, J. (1980), *Practical Corporate Planning*, George Allen & Unwin.

Argyris, C. (1964), *Integrating the Individual and the Organisation*, John Wiley.

Attwood, M. (1989), *Personnel Management*, Macmillan.

Burns, T. and Stalker, G. (1971), *The Management of Innovation*, Tavistock Publications.

Campbell, J. P., Dunnett, M. D., Lawler, E. E. and Weick, K. (1970), *Managerial Behavior, Performance and Effectiveness*, McGraw-Hill.

Carnall, C. and Maxwell, S. (1988), *Management: Principles and Policy*, ICSA Publishing.

Child, J. (1984), *Organization: A Guide to Problems and Practice*, Harper & Row.

Clarke, P. (1972), *Small Businesses – How They Survive and Succeed*, David & Charles.

Cole, G. A. (1983), *Personnel Management: Theory and Practice*, D. P. Publications.

Cyert, R. M. and March, J. G. (1963), *A Behavioural Theory of the Firm*, Prentice-Hall.

Drucker, P. F. (1968), *The Practice of Management*, Pan Books.

Emery, F. E. and Trist, E. L. (1965), 'The causal texture of organisational environments', *Human Relations*, February.

Fiedler, F. E. (1967), *A Theory of Leadership Effectiveness*, McGraw-Hill.

Handy, C. (1984), *Understanding Organizations*, Penguin.

Herzberg, F., Mausner, B. and Synderman, B. (1960), *The Motivation to Work*, John Wiley.

Howe, W. S. (1986), *Corporate Strategy*, Macmillan.

Humble, J. W. (1972), *Improving Business Results*, Pan Books.

Kast, F. E. and Rosenzweig, J. E. (1974), *Organization and Management: A Systems Approach*, McGraw-Hill.

Lawler, E. E. (1978), *Motivation and Work Organizations*, Brooks Cole Free Press.

Lawrence, P. R. And Lorsch, J. (1967), *Organization and Environment*, Richard D. Irwin.

McGregor, D. (1960), *The Human Side of Enterprise*, McGraw-Hill.

March, J. G. and Simon, H. A. (1958), *Organization*, John Wiley.

Maslow, A. H. (1970), *Motivation and Personality*, Harper & Row.

Mintzberg, H. (1973), *The Nature of Managerial Work*, Harper & Row.

Reddin, W. J. (1970), *Managerial Effectiveness*, McGraw-Hill.

Rees, W. D. (1984), *The Skills of Management*, Croom Helm.

Revans, R. W. (1971), *Developing Effective Managers: A New Approach to Business Education*, Longman.

Rodger, A. (1970), *The Seven Point Plan*, National Institute of Industrial Psychology.

Simon, H. A. (1957), *Administrative Behaviour*, Macmillan.

Stewart, R. (1970), *Managers and Their Jobs*, Macmillan.

Stewart, R. (1979), *The Reality of Management*, Pan Books.

Storey, D. J. (1982), *Entrepreneurship and the New Firm*, Croom Helm.

Tavsky, C. and Parke, E. L. (1976), 'Job enrichment, need theory and reinforcement theory'; in Dublin, R. (ed) *Handbook of Work*, *Organizations and Society*, Rand McNally.

Urwick, L. (1952), *Notes on the Theory of Organization*, American Management Association.

Urwick, L. (1958), *The Elements of Administration*, Pitman.

Vroom, V. H. (1964), *Work and Motivation*, John Wiley.

Woodward, J. (1965), *Industrial Organization: Theory and Practice*, Oxford University Press.

Yetton, P. W. and Vroom, V. H. (1978) 'The Vroom–Yetton model of leadership – an overview'; in King, B., Strenfert, S. and Fiedler, F. E. (eds) *Managerial Control and Organizational Democracy*, John Wiley.

Index